HYEM

(YEM, HJEM, HOME)

by PHILIP CORREIA

Published by Playdead Press 2017

© Philip Correia 2017

Philip Correia has asserted his rights under the Copyright, Design and Patents Act, 1988, to be identified as the authors of this work.

A CIP catalogue record for this book is available from the British Library.

ISBN 978-1-910067-54-3

Playdead Press
www.playdeadpress.com

NorthSEE THEATRE in association with
Theatre503 present

HYEM

by PHILIP CORREIA

First performed at Theatre503, Battersea, London
on August 30th 2017

HYEM

CAST

SYLV	Charlie Hardwick
MICK	Patrick Driver
LAURA	Aimée Kelly
DUMMEY	Ryan Nolan
SHELLEY	Sarah Balfour
DEAN	Joe Blakemore

CREATIVE

Director	Jonny Kelly
Designer	Jasmine Swan
Lighting Designer	Peter Harrison
Sound Designer	Richard Bell
Production Manager	Alistair Borland
Stage Manager	Tomos Derrick
Producer	Emma Murton

CAST

Charlie Hardwick | Sylv

Charlie is best known for playing the role of Val Pollard in *Emmerdale* for 11 years - during this time she won the award for Best Comedy Performance, Best On-Screen Partnership and Best Exit.

She has performed in over 50 productions across the length and breadth of the country including Lee Hall's *Cooking With Elvis* and Karin Young's *The Awkward Squad* in the West End; *Romeo and Juliet* at York Theatre Royal; *Dick Wittington* at Newcastle's Theatre Royal; *Peter Pan* at The Alhambra, Bradford; *The Snow Queen*, *Beauty and The Beast*, *Foreign Lands* at Northern Stage; *Bandits*, *A Nightingale Sang*, *Your Home in The West* with Live Theatre Co, where she also gave an award-winning performance as the Emcee in *Cabaret*.

Her film credits include *Purely Belter*, *Billy Elliot* and *The Scar*, for which she won best actress at Monte Carlo Film and TV awards. She also spent four years as Sian in *Byker Grove*, and appeared in many TV series and dramas including *Eastenders*, *Casualty*, *Different For Girls*, *Our Friends In The North*, *The Royal*, *See You Friday*, and Catherine Cookson's *Tide of Life* and *Colour Blind*.

She has many radio plays to her credit and is the voice of Iris Reed in Radio 4's epic World War 1 drama, *Home Front*. Charlie has been a regular on Loose Women, a presenter for BBC local Television and Radio, and sings in a brilliant band of women called Kissed back home in the North-East.

Patrick Driver | Mick

Theatre includes: *Tale of Two Cities* (Regent's Park), *Educating Rita* (Gala Theatre, Durham), *The Herbal Bed* (ETT/Royal and Derngate/Rose), *Measure for Measure, As You Like It, The Heresy of Love, Julius Caesar, Dr. Scroggy's War, The Taming of the Shrew* (Shakespeare's Globe Theatre), *Faith Healer* (Lyceum, Edinburgh), *The Curious Incident of the Dog in the Night-time* (West End) *For Once* (Hampstead, Traverse, UK tour), *Bus Stop* (New Vic & Scarborough SJT), *Treasure Island* (Watermill), *Faith Healer, Othello, Drowning on Dry Land* (Salisbury Playhouse), *Ma Rainey's Black Bottom, London Assurance, Volpone* (Royal Exchange Manchester), *Reverence – A Tale of Abelard & Heloise* (Southwark Playhouse), *No, It Was You* (Arcola Theatre), As actor and Joint-Artistic Director of Dialogue Productions, he has appeared in *Scorched (*Old Vic Tunnels), *Top Dogs* (Southwark Playhouse & UK tour), and was assistant director on their production of *Monsieur Ibrahim and The Flowers of the Qur'an* (Bush Theatre, Edinburgh and tour).

Television includes: *Call the Midwife, Guerilla, Silent Witness, EastEnders, Friday Night Dinner, Whistleblowers, Peepshow Holby City, Doctors, The Bill, The Office, The Last Chancers, Worst Week of My Life, Grass,, People Like Us, My Hero, Ghosts and Mr Charity.*

Aimée Kelly | Laura

Aimée made her screen debut aged 16 playing the lead in feature film *Sket*. The film premiered as part of the 55th BFI London Film Festival. For her performance, Aimée was nominated for Best British Newcomer at the LFF Awards.

On television, Aimée lead the cast in the first and second series of fantasy drama *Wolfblood* for CBBC. For her performance as Maddy Smith, Aimée was nominated for the award for best performer at the 2013 Children's BAFTAs.

Other credits include: *Call the Midwife* (BBC); *Care* (Sky Arts).

Ryan Nolan | Dummey

Ryan is from Newcastle and recently graduated from Project A at Newcastle's Theatre Royal. At Project A he played Skinlad and Eddie in *Road*, Les in Berkoff's *East*, Benedick in *Much Ado About Nothing* and Tom in *Citizenship*. Ryan has also appeared in some short films including Adrift, Random Acts and Vandals, BFI Film Academy. *Hyem* is Ryan's professional stage debut.

Sarah Balfour | Shelley

Sarah Balfour is originally from Newcastle, where she studied at Newcastle College. She went on to study a BA in Acting at the Academy of Live and Recorded Art, which she graduated from with a First Class Honours this July. During her studies, Sarah received high praise from director Dickon Tyrrell for her performance of Ophelia in *Hamlet*. Her performance of Dean in play *Pronoun* as part of the National Theatre Connections Scheme was a stand-out to the panel and the production was given a Diversity Award. In addition to this, Sarah writes and performs her own spoken word pieces. Her work was selected to be presented at feminist festival HERSTORY 2 at Theatre N16, as well as the 'Scratch Me If You Can' event which took place at the 2016 Vaults Festival.

Joe Blakemore | Dean

Joe Blakemore is a London based actor from Newcastle Upon Tyne. Joe graduated from RADA in 2014. *Hyem* is Joes' debut stage play. Appearances in film and TV: *The Levelling, Next of Kin, Stan Lee's Lucky Man, Vera, Banged Up Abroad, The Drug Trial: Emergency at the Hospital, Trolley Boy* and *Doctors*.

CREATIVE

Jonny Kelly | Director

Jonny Kelly is Assistant Director of Papatango Theatre Company and has trained at East 15 Acting School. Direction includes *Proud* (Finborough Theatre), *A is for Ali* (Old Red Lion Theatre), *Money Womb* (Theatre503), *The Special Relationship* (Southwark Playhouse), *Boys Will Be Boys* (Soho Theatre), *Lies* (VAULT Festival), and *Call Centre* (New Wimbledon Theatre). Associate and Assistant Direction includes assisting Justin Audibert on *Flare Path* (National Tour) and Nina Raine on *Donkey Heart* (Trafalgar Studios), *The Hard Man* and *Unscorched* (Finborough Theatre).

Philip Correia | Playwright

Hyem (yem, hjem, home) is Philip Correia's debut play. A member of the Orange Tree Writer's Collective and Papatango Prize runner up, Philip has had rehearsed readings at NT Studio & Live! Theatre Newcastle. He is best known for his acting work at the NT, regionally and in the West End. He has worked in television, in film, radio and in video games.

Jasmine Swan | Designer

Jasmine studied Theatre Performance Design at Liverpool Institute for Performing Arts, graduating in 2016 with a First-Class BA Hons. She is very hands on with the design process having experience in: Scenic Art, Costume Props, Puppetry and Prop making.

Her recent design credits include:

Scene Change Presents: Coming of Age (Liverpool Playhouse Studio), *Who's Afraid Of The Working Class?* (Unity Theatre), *The Wonderful World of Dissocia* (Liverpool Playhouse Studio), *Next Door But One* and *Animal Farm* (both for Tell Tale Theatre Company).

Peter Harrison | Lighting Designer

Trained at RADA, graduating in December 1999 with an Honours Diploma in Stage Electrics. Lighting design work has ranged from the pub theatres of the London Fringe through national and international touring to West End productions. He also works as a Production Electrician and notable productions include *Jerusalem*, *Clybourne Park*, *Posh*, *Mojo* and *Who's Afraid of Virginia Woolf, Three Days of Rain, Pinter's People, Under the Blue Sky* all in the West End, and *Decade* at St Katharine's Dock. *Minetti* at the Edinburgh International Festival *Giselle* and *Rian* in Poland and Galway.

As a Relighter, his credits include productions for Shared Experience, Donmar Warehouse, Headlong, Oxford Stage Company, The Lyric Hammersmith and Grange Park Opera, for Lighting Designers such as Paule Constable, Jon Clark, Adam Silverman, Chris Davey and Natasha Chivers.

Richard Bell | Sound Design

Theatre as Sound Designer: *Windows* (Finborough Theatre), MA Directors' Festival (Orange Tree Theatre), *Birthday Suit* (Old Red Lion Theatre), *Wet Bread* (Sheer Drop), *Further. Still, Nailhouse* (Old Red Lion Theatre).

Theatre as Associate Sound Designer: *My Eyes Went Dark* (59E59, New York), *1984* (Playhouse Theatre and Australian Tour), *The Lottery of Love, Blue Heart* (Orange Tree Theatre), *We're Stuck* (China Plate / One Tenth Human), *Frankenstein* (Watermill Theatre, Wilton's Music Hall), *Years of Sunlight* (Theatre503), *The Children* (Royal Court), *Peter Pan Goes Wrong* (Apollo Theatre), *I Call My Brothers, Diary of a Madman, The Iphigenia Quartet* (Gate Theatre), *The Sugar-Coated Bullets of the Bourgeoisie* (Arcola / HighTide), *A High Street Odyssey* (Inspector Sands).

Alistair Borland | Production Manager

Alastair is a degree-qualified Theatre Technician (E15 Acting School) with experience in Lighting, Sound, Stage Management and Production Management. He is the current Technical Manager at Theatre 503 in London and has primarily worked in venues across London and the South East.

Previous credits include: Lighting design – *Top Trumps* (Theatre 503), *Midsummer Night's Dream* (Waterloo East Theatre), *Caught* (Pleasance Theatre London), *Saucy Jack and the Space Vixens* (Komedia Brighton), *Yesterdays Tomorrow* (Drayton Arms Theatre). Sound design: *Top Trumps* (Theatre 503), *Othello* (Barons Court Theatre).

Tomos Derrick | Stage Manager

A recent graduated from LAMDA SMTT (2015 – 2017) Tomos is ex-cited to be involved in *HYEM (yem, hjem, home)* and work with NorthSEE Theatre.

Emma Murton | Producer

Emma is a founding director of NorthSEE Theatre. Originally from Somerset, Emma is a Stage One producer who recently was assistant producer on *Run The Beast Down* starring Ben Aldridge, at the Finborough Theatre, London, for Libby Brodie Productions, which received three Offie nominations. She has worked within regional and London theatre including ATG, Opera Holland Park, The Marlowe Theatre and The Gulbenkian. Producing credits include: *Voices of The Great War* (Theatre Royal Brighton), *Macbeth* (Canterbury Shakespeare Festival), *Two Nobel Kinsmen* (Mirthful Oak Theatre) and *Agatha Christie's The Rats* (Canterbury Festival).

NORTHSEE
theatre

We create new theatre, from unheard voices.
We support artists from across the country.
We leave audiences speechless.

NorthSEE Theatre is a company founded by producer
Emma Murton and Director Jonny Kelly and is dedicated to
making high quality productions that showcase regional
talent in and around London.

We are supported by the English Touring Theatre as one of
their Forge companies. This offers us unique insight into
producing theatre for a London and regional audience –
alongside gaining advice, support and provisions as up-
coming theatre makers.

www.northseetheatre.com
Twitter: @northseetheatre
Facebook: /northseetheatre
Email: northseetheatre@gmail.com

Supported using public funding by
**ARTS COUNCIL
ENGLAND**

THEATRE 503

Theatre503 is a 60-seat new writing powerhouse situated in the heart of Battersea, South London. It launches the work of more new writers than any other theatre in the UK and is the smallest theatre in the world to have won an Olivier award (for Katori Hall's *The Mountaintop*). Playwrights whose careers started at the theatre include Tom Morton Smith (*Oppenheimer*), Anna Jordan (*Yen*), Dennis Kelly (*Matilda the Musical*) and Katori Hall (*Photograph 51*).

Theatre503 would not be successful without the amazing support we receive from our dedicated team of volunteers:
Kelly Agredo, Rosie Akerman, Serafina Cusack, Mark Doherty, Bridget Rudder, Darren Siah, Rob Ellis, Tom Hartwell, George Linfield, Mike Murgaz, Mandy Nicholls, Annabel Pemberton, Andrei Vornicu, Emily Standring, Simon Mander, Mike McGarry, Phoebe Hyder, Nicole Zweiback, Suzanne Brewis, Nathalie Czarnecki, Emma Griffiths, Asha Osborne, Carla Kingham, Emma Griffiths and Aydan Tair.

OUR SUPPORTERS
We are incredibly grateful to the following who have supported us recently without whom our work would not be possible:
The Harold Hyman Wingate Foundation, The Schroder Charity Trust, The Boris Karloff Foundation, The Idelwild Trust, Cockayne Grants for the Arts, The Peter Wolff Trust, The Sylvia Waddilove Foundation, The Thistle Trust, The Unity Theatre Trust, The Williams Trust, The Audience Club, M&G Investments, Barbara Broccoli, Wandsworth Council, Arts Council England Grants for the Arts, all our Friends, Patrons and Point of Sale Donors.

We are currently in receipt of funding from Arts Council England's Catalyst Evolve fund – allowing us to grow our fundraising capacity by match funding income from new donors over the next three years. Particular thanks to the Richard Carne Trust for their generous support of our Playwriting Award and 503 Five.

NORTHERN STAGE

Northern Stage is the largest producing theatre company in the North East of England, and one of the top-eleven producing theatres in the UK. As well as our work in Newcastle, you might see us out on tour around the country with some of our biggest work, and at the Edinburgh Fringe Festival with our temporary venues at St Stephen's, King's Hall and Summerhall.

We have built a reputation for fresh and relevant productions of modern classics that attract audiences of all ages, including Joseph Heller's hilarious satire *Catch-22*, Edward Albee's razor-sharp *Who's Afraid of Virginia Woolf?*, the Geordie epics *Close The Coalhouse Door* and *Our Friends in the North*, a 1950s version of Henrik Ibsen's *A Doll's House*, Angela Carter's *The Bloody Chamber* and the landmark satirical musical *Oh What A Lovely War*. We're also committed to families in the north-east and every year produce two new Christmas shows; past productions include *Get Santa, A Christmas Carol, Thumbelina, The Wind in the Willows, The Borrowers* and *Get Santa*.

Besides producing our own work, we are dedicated to presenting the best in local, national and international theatre. Since reopening in 2006 we have hosted the likes of Frantic Assembly, Kneehigh Theatre, Headlong Theatre, DV8 Physical Theatre, The Opera Group, the National Theatre of Scotland and the Royal Shakespeare Company.

Our Creative Residencies programme gives resources to local theatre-makers to develop and present their work in our theatre and frequently you'll find emerging and developing artists using our spaces and creating work throughout the venue.

NorthSEE Theatre would like to thank the entire cast and creative team, all those at Theatre503, Northern Stage and English Touring Theatre especially Andrew Shepherd, Lisa Spirling and Jane Claire as well as the following people, all of whom have supported this production: Arts Council England, Kim Murton, Marc Elliot, Owain Arthur, Liam Wilkinson, Katie Catling, Chris Foxon, Will Wrightson, Lisa Blair, Mel Hilyard, Nadia Fall, The Orange Tree Writer's Collective, Live! Theatre Newcastle, Lorne Campbell, Kenny Wax, Peter Flannery, Jeremy Conway, Sam O'Mahony, 6 Degree Media, Shelagh Stephenson, Kara Fitzpatrick, Nathan Capone, Tom Iverson, the Young Vic & Jessica Campbell.

The author would like to thank all of the above plus Jane Eltringham, Maureen Curry, Anne and Nicky Hunter, The People's Theatre, The Phoenix Theatre, Dave Grey, the casts of both readings of this play, the Ward family and all of his parents and family.

This play is for Alice, Adam, Marc and David.   With thanks.

HYEM *(Yem, Hjem, Home)*
by Philip Correia

Hyem, Noun; place of family, sanctuary and comfort;

adverb: "I'm gannin' hyem" – I'm going home.

(Geordie/Old English/Scandinavian)

The Play is set on 'Fountain Park' Estate, in the North East of England, in February 2003.

Every scene is in MICK AND SYLV'S living room. There is no interval.

CHARACTERS:

SYLV

MICK

LAURA

DUMMEY

SHELLEY

DEAN

SCENE 1

ALAN DUMMETT or 'DUMMEY', 13, is pale, short and skinny. The type of boy that needs his neck washed. He is dressed in a school uniform, trainers and a tracksuit top.

A smoke-stained LIVING ROOM. A stuffed owl hangs near the entrance, a ship's wheel on the wall. A large blue tit statue. A taxidermic menagerie. A photograph of a 1973 blue convertible Porsche 911s. Young men in Navy uniform. An animal hide rug. On the hearth; a replica Viking helmet and a lurid mermaid statue. There is a sword. There is a tank containing a LIVE PYTHON. There are tequila bottles containing worms, sex aids, shisha pipes. There is a door to the KITCHEN. There is a staircase. There is a window with net curtains.

DUMMEY, anxious, with his hands in his pockets, stands facing the audience, waiting. He hears someone move at the top of the stairs.

DUMMEY: Laura?

DUMMEY is shocked as DEAN appears walking down the stairs. DEAN, 20's, looks dangerous, tall and imposing. He has a blue tear tattooed to his face. DUMMEY registers this.

DUMMEY: Alreet.

Ignoring him, DEAN, walks over to the PYTHON. DUMMEY stares at him. DEAN feeds the snake a MOUSE. He carefully opens the lid of the tank. He places the MOUSE in the tank and strokes the SNAKE. He closes the lid. He turns sharply towards DUMMEY. DUMMEY looks away. DEAN exits as abruptly as he arrived.

DUMMEY: Charming.

*DUMMEY awkward.   He tries the TV using a remote control.
Loud white noise.   He presses again.   The Video plays.   It's a soft
porn film.*

DUMMEY: Woah.

*DUMMEY hears a noise from behind him.   Panicking, he tries
to turn off the TV and in trying to do so knocks over a Viking
helmet.   He dives to save it.   From behind his back, SYLV, early
60s, enters from the KITCHEN.   She is authoritative, tough,
careful, knowledgeable.*

SYLV: Put that down.

DUMMEY doesn't move.

SYLV: I said put it down.

He does.

SYLV: What do you want? Money? We've plenty.
                    You can take it and fuck off.

DUMMEY: I'm not a thief.

She acknowledges the TV.

SYLV: Or is it sex?

DUMMEY: What?

SYLV: You're here to have sex with me?

DUMMEY: Eh?

SYLV: Insert your penis into my vagina?

DUMMEY: NO!

SYLV: Turn around. Slowly.

He does.

SYLV: I don't know you.

DUMMEY shakes his head.

SYLV: Why don't I know you?

DUMMEY: 'cause we've never met?

SYLV: (*Unimpressed. In her bag.*) Hmm.

DUMMEY: Divin't call the busies.

SYLV: I wouldn't dream of it.

SYLV takes out cig/make up? Beat. DUMMEY seizes the moment to go.

DUMMEY: Gotta go.

SYLV: You'll stay exactly where you are.

DUMMEY: What're ye gonna dee to 'is?

SYLV: Depends. The big man's on his way.

Beat

I'd start praying if I were you.

DUMMEY: The big man?

Looks to stairs.

SYLV: Our Dean's upstairs. So I'd say you're in a bit of a tight spot.

DUMMEY: I.

SYLV: You won't make trouble here.

DUMMEY: I w/on't

SYLV: / What have you heard?

DUMMEY: Noth/ing.

SYLV: You can't just turn up. We don't have uninvited guests here. Do you understand?

DUMMEY: I was invited.

SYLV: Oh really?

Behind SYLV, LAURA, 16, enters down the staircase in SYLV's Chinese dressing gown.

LAURA: (*Alluring*) Dummey... (*Surprised*) Shit. Sylv! When did you get back?

SYLV: Never mind when I got back, I'm here now.

LAURA: I didn't expect you.

SYLV: Evidently. Do you know this...

LAURA: Yeah.

SYLV: (*Sharp*) Why don't I know him?

LAURA: You do. Course you do. I told you about him. Dummey.

SYLV: Dummey?

LAURA: Dummey.

DUMMEY: Dummey.

SYLV:	'Dummey'. Let's just keep saying it. Bound to make sense eventually. Why are you watching pornography Dummey?
DUMMEY:	I couldn't get it off.
SYLV:	Unlucky for some. (*Switches it off first time.*) Porn and politics. All that's ever on in this house. Any more surprises for me Laura?

SHELLEY, 16, appears from the cupboard under the stairs. SHELLEY, speaks bluntly, directly and flatly, unremitting honesty. She doesn't do subtle, lies and struggles to access emotion.

SHELLEY:	Aright Sylv. I was in the cupboard.
SYLV:	Shelley!
SHELLEY:	I had to move the telly.
SYLV:	Would someone like to explain why we've all decided to behave like lunatics today?
SHELLEY:	We brought Dummey round to meet you, but then we thought you were out, so Laura asked Dummey if he wanted to see her blue bra. I think he was turned on.

DUMMEY is bright red.

SYLV:	Are you turned on? (*To SHELLEY*) I cannot tell. Gan on.
SHELLEY:	I was in the cupboard. For protection.
SYLV:	Wouldn't a johnny've been more use?
SHELLEY:	In case Dummey got. Frisky.

SYLV: (*To SHELLEY*) What have I told you about taking your shoes off? You'll have mud all ower me rug.

SHELLEY: (*Sitting and removing her shoes*) Sorry Sylv.

SYLV: You're lucky Mick's not here mind.

GIRLS: Sorry Sylv.

SYLV: Mick might have killed this young man.

DUMMEY: What?

SYLV: Laura have you done your papers? Blank face. Do you want them calling your mother? I don't. You can nick us a Chron, Mick'll want ees Morning Star and mind you put me dressing gown back properly.

LAURA: Yes Sylv. Sorry Sylv. (*Sultry*) Excuse me Dummey.

LAURA exits. SYLV rolls her eyes.

SHELLEY: You should sit down Dummey. It makes people uncomfortable when you hover about.

SYLV: Aye sit down and stop all this hovering about.

DUMMEY sits.

SYLV: Who are you?

An interview.

SHELLEY: Dummey.

SYLV: Not this again.

SHELLEY: Alan Dummett. He's the one I told ye about. From the fight. I told him if he came, you'd give him a tab and let him see the snake. As a reward.

SYLV: We'll have to ask the big man about that. And I suspect 'he' can speak for hesel'. You can speak for yoursel' can you? Or are you so mesmerized by Laura's allure, you've forgotten how?

DUMMEY: Yeah. No.

DUMMEY goes pink. He squirms at the powerful women that surround him.

SYLV: Don't be coy. Where do you live?

Beat as DUMMEY looks at SHELLEY. DUMMEY is lonely as opposed to shy. He hasn't been asked to speak before.

SHELLEY: He lives the other side of the ressy.

SYLV: Shelley get your tongue out ees mouth.

DUMMEY: Ugh.

SHELLEY: He'll never speak Sylv. Ees like this at school.

SYLV: Is that right Dummey? (*DUMMEY shrugs*) Whey this's gonna be a lang old chat then isn't it? Can I ask where you live?

SHELLEY: Foundlin' Street.

SYLV: (*look to Shelley*) And you live with your Mam and Dad?

SHELLEY: He lives with ees Mam, ees sister Chloe and sometimes ees dad. But he doesn't really live there.

DUMMEY: Kev's not me Dad.

SYLV: Kev?

DUMMEY: (*Back to mumbles*) Mam's friend.

SYLV: Oh, I see. Kev's your Mam's friend. Do they know you're here now?

DUMMEY shakes his head.

SYLV: I see. Won't they worry?

DUMMEY: (*beat*) Nur.

SYLV: Hmm?

DUMMEY: No.

SYLV: Hope not. I hear you've been in a bit of mischief?

DUMMEY looks aghast. Looks at SHELLEY.

SYLV: (*with a shrug*) I like naughty boys.

SHELLEY: He was getting bullied.

DUMMEY: I wasn't.

SHELLEY: He ran away for three days.

DUMMEY: Shelley man.

SHELLEY: If you weren't getting bullied why did you have to come to our school?

SYLV: That's enough Shelley.

SHELLEY: He definitely was. And he got arrested.

DUMMEY: Shelley. Shut up.

SYLV: A fugitive? How exciting. (*beat*) And you're friends with Shelley and Laura are ye pet?

DUMMEY: (*unsure*) Suppose.

SHELLEY: You don't have any others.

SYLV: I've heard all about your heroics. Punched that lad, picking on Laura again.

DUMMEY: Did I?

SHELLEY: You went psycho.

SYLV: That's what I heard. Just walked ower and punched him right on the beak. Ee Laura was very grateful wasn't she Shel'?

SHELLEY: She didn't ask him to do it.

SYLV: He sounds quite a nasty piece of work this boy?

SHELLEY: Scotty skulls? He's a proper mentalist.

DUMMEY: Is he?

SHELLEY: She should've let me rip ees balls off. Cos now Scotty's gonna wait for Dummey every day after school and when he sees him, he's gonna spark 'im spark out.

SYLV: Thank you, Shelley.

SHELLEY: He says he's gonna chin him so hard/ that ees brains…

SYLV: /Thank you pet. Is there nothing else to do in the North East these days?

SHELLEY: No Sylv. There's nowt.

SYLV: (*exasperated at Shelley*) Well we know a few nasty people ourselves. How's about I ask our Dean to have a chat with this Scotty Skips?

SHELLEY: Skulls.

SYLV: Aha. And Shelley'll fetch you the cigs you wanted.

SHELLEY: Can he not stay?

SYLV: Fetch the tabs will you pet?

DUMMEY disappointed, head bowed. SHELLEY gets up during the pause, gives cigs to DUMMEY.

DUMMEY: Nice to meet you.

SYLV: Pleasure's all mine pet.

DUMMEY: Yer house is dead nice.

SYLV: Well thank you. (*Smiles*) You're a good looking boy when you look up. How old are you?

DUMMEY: Fourteen /

SHELLEY: / Thirteen

SYLV: Thirteen going on fourteen? Bit old for me then. Popular with the girls? Or the boys?

DUMMEY: Not really. Not popular with anyone really.

SYLV: Get away.

DUMMEY: Honestly. I wish.

SYLV: (*laughs. DUMMEY smiles. She studies him*) Very charming. (*big change of tone*) Ee by God. Michael. That smile. Like that.

SHELLEY: Ee Sylv. He is ye kna.

SYLV: The spit. Ee God.

DUMMEY: What?

Beat.

SYLV: Well I never. Michael Dobson. (*beat*) Here you are pet.

SYLV retrieves a lighter and hands it to DUMMEY. They all light up.

DUMMEY: Thanks.

SYLV: Take your shoes off then. If you're stayin'.

DUMMEY does so. Begins to relax a fraction. Is he ok to stay? LAURA descends the stairs with paper bag, she dresses extraordinarily despite the uniform. DUMMEY straightens up.

LAURA: See you on Shelley.

SHELLEY: Aye see you on Laura.

LAURA: See you on Sylv.

28

SYLV: Aye see you on pet.

LAURA: See you later 'Ali'.

DUMMEY: Erm. Bye.

She leaves. DUMMEY looks to SHELLEY for an explanation.

SHELLEY: The boxer.

Pause. DUMMEY looks around the room again. Taking it all in. SYLV's eyes follow him like a hawk.

SYLV: I spy with my little eye. (*DUMMEY sees the snake*) Something beginning with. Python. Say hello. She mightn't bite. You won't last long to worry about it if she does. Shy bairns get nowt.

DUMMEY anxiously approaches the case. His face nears the glass. The snake darts across the case. Yelping, DUMMEY staggers back in fright, tripping on the hide rug. At this precise moment MICK bursts into the LIVING ROOM from the KITCHEN, slamming the door on CLARK GABLE, a large, snarling, German Shepherd. MICK, a powerful man in his 60's, looks like he has taken a lot of drugs in his youth. He wears boots and a donkey jacket. He has Naval and prison tattoos on his hands and neck. He has the air of a military man. He has a shaved head. He is intimidating with kind eyes. He is a whirlwind of bluster. A born entertainer, everything for effect. Loud. A force of nature. He speaks very quickly, like a machine gun.

MICK: What the ruddy hell's goin' on here? Lying about on my ruddy good rug? You think this is Miami 90210?

DUMMEY: Sorry?

29

MICK:　　　　Speak up.

DUMMEY:　　It was the snake do you know what I mean?

MICK:　　　　Do I know what you mean? Do I know what you mean? (*to SHELLEY*) This is typical ruddy Blair generation. Talk in riddles all of 'em. What do you mean?

DUMMEY:　　The snake.

MICK:　　　　You were talkin' to the snake? Jesus. Who are you then? David Attenborough? What were you saying then snake charmer?

DUMMEY:　　I'm not a charmer.

MICK:　　　　You said it kid. You can barely speak. Hardly surprising mind. Teachers being shackled. Ruddy league tables.

SYLV:　　　　Mick! He's only a young'un

MICK:　　　　Well this is it Sylvie, my lovely lover, this is precisely my point. These young lads don't know who they ruddy well are. Ha' you seen the News? It's a ruddy crusade he's on. Universal ruddy values? Look at 'em. When I was a young buck I was out there. On the streets. Wapping. Brixton. ON the ruddy picket. Look at 'em now, Blair generation. Too ruddy comfortable. This country's funeral bell's already rung. A Blair generation if ever I saw one.

DUMMEY:　　Bear what?

30

MICK:	(*turns on a sixpence to anger*) You deaf now as well? What you doin' in my house?
DUMMEY:	What?
MICK:	(*jovial again*) Ears have gone again.
DUMMEY:	I won't be any trouble.
MICK:	(*turns again*) You're right boy. Fuck off.
DUMMEY:	Sorry?
MICK:	(*threat*) Get out, before I break your legs.
DUMMEY:	Sorry.
MICK:	Sorry? Sorry? (*searches his pockets*) Why? What've you stolen?
DUMMEY:	(*with considerable spirit*) Nothing man. Get off us or I'll knock y'out.

MICK catches DUMMEY's flying fist, turns him over. Surprised. Beat.

SYLV:	Mickey. This young man was invited.
MICK:	(*holding DUMMEY*) Invited?
	(*to SHELLEY*) Invited?

SHELLEY nods.

MICK:	A new recruit? Alright young'un. Riddle me this and you're off the hook. Who is Tony Benn?
DUMMEY:	Tony...

MICK:	Benn.
DUMMEY:	(*after a beat*) The chicken sauce guy?
MICK:	(*beat. Loud laughter*) That is classic my lad. Classic. Let's do this properly. I'm o'ny teasing. It's just me isn't it Sylv?
SYLV:	Don't we know it. Bliddy Billy Connolly.
MICK:	Now who have we got here?
SHELLEY:	Dummey.
MICK:	Dummey? Jesus. Dummey? Like a ruddy rubber nipple? Dummey? What a cruel joke that is. That is blumin' cruel o' your mother. You must have a real name son?
DUMMEY:	Alan. Alan Dummett.
MICK:	Private Alan Dummett. (*salutes*) Corporal Mickey Dobson, that young thing is sexy Sylvie, the love of my life and I presume you know that beauty at 11 o'clock is Shel'. Welcome to our squad. Now 'ow did you wind up here then?
DUMMEY:	I was invited. Shelley. And Laura.
MICK:	Laura as well eh. Ooh he's eyes lit up there. Sparkled like the ruddy light'ouse when he mentioned our Laura. We'll sort you out lad.
SYLV:	Dummey is the young man who stepped in when Laura was in trouble.
MICK:	Tough lad eh? So I'd noticed. But no one fights in this house. Y'understand?

DUMMEY: OK.

MICK: But this was different? (*playing an English noble*) Defending a lady's honour like a noble sporting champ. Eh? (*he starts boxing, playing Ali*) Moves like a ruddy butterfly, stings like a ruddy bee! Ah! Ooh!

DUMMEY is encouraged to box. He tries hard. MICK plays roughly with him.

MICK: He's short but he's ruddy angry! Got you!

DUMMEY: Get off 'is man! Ah that tickles.

MICK: Not short on looks either. Spirit 'n' looks. There's a proper proposition. (*of himself*) Remind you of anyone Darlin'? I can see in your eyes you're a find my lad.

He stops. Urgent.

DUMMEY: What? What have I done?

MICK: Is this a joke?

DUMMEY: I'm sorry. Have I done something?

MICK: (*beat. To SYLV*) Is this? (*to DUMMEY, smiles after a beat*) Blow me. Nothing bonny lad. I just caught a glimpse o' those peepers o' yours. I was ruddy transfixed.

SYLV: Mickey.

MICK: Hmm?

SYLV: You OK?

MICK: Never better my darling. Never better.

He strides over and kisses SYLV.

SYLV: (*surprised and delighted in equal measure*) Oh.

MICK: I am A OK.

SYLV: I see that.

MICK: Special kid.

CLARK barks like mad.

MICK: CLARK! (*to Dummey, whispering like Elmer Fudd*) He's spied a wabbit. (*normal volume*) A more sunny disposition in a dog there never was. Pure old labour that dog.

SYLV: Can smell a tory a mile off! Go in and see. He does. We hear 'Good boy' etc. Barks.

MICK: (*shouting*) I tell you what lad, he likes you and he's got excellent taste has Clark Gable.

DUMMEY: (*back in*) I like Clark Gable.

SYLV: It's nice to hear you pipe up.

DUMMEY: I like dogs. You's've got loads of photos. (*picking one up, it's a naked woman*) WHOA. Who's that?

MICK: Ha ha. That's her son. (*indicating SYLV*) Beautiful, isn't she? (*DUMMEY blushes*) You can have that if you like.

SYLV: Ee ee'll never sleep again! (*to LAURA*) Be good for ees arms mind you.

MICK: Alright, alright. What about this girl. More your style?

He removes one of the pictures of the Porsche from the wall.

DUMMEY: Wow. Ace. 911 isn't it?

MICK: (*whispering to SYLV*) It's Jeremy Clarkson. (*looking at the image*) Gorgeous isn't she? 1973 Blue 911 Convertible. Cannot beat her.

DUMMEY: Can I see her?

SYLV: I think Mickey's showing off a bit.

MICK: You don't like it? (*winks at SYLV. Then; of the Porsche*) She's in the garage in her PJ and Duncans son. Now Sylvia platter of joy, any tea for a hungry old man?

DUMMEY: Oh shit, what time is it? Me Mam'll bray us if I'm late.

SYLV: You don't bring bother here. Your mother at my door doesn't happen. Understand? (*relaxing*) Mickey, can we supply this young man with some tabs?

MICK: Hm yeah I think I could manage that.

SYLV: (*winks*) Would you help me reach them down Mickey darling?

MICK and SYLV go into the KITCHEN, as SHELLEY and SYLV exchange a pointed glance. SHELLEY lights up as they put on their shoes to go.

SHELLEY: You said you were me friend.

DUMMEY: Eh?

SHELLEY: You said we were friends. To Sylv.

DUMMEY: Did I?

SHELLEY: Don't bother speaking t'ris at school.

DUMMEY: Oh.

SHELLEY: Not that you've got anyone else to speak to.

DUMMEY: Shut up. Couple that? (*of the cigarette*) Ugh. What's wi these?

SHELLEY: They're menthol.

DUMMEY: They're minging. It's like airy chewing gum.

SHELLEY: Aye. Got bits of mint in them. S'healthier.

DUMMEY: Where they from like?

SHELLEY: Continental. Tenerife I think.

DUMMEY: Does everyone at school kna why I moved schools?

SHELLEY: Everyone.

DUMMEY: What do people say?

SHELLEY: The' think you might do a columbo (*pronounced like columbine*)

DUMMEY: Eh?

SHELLEY: Shoot everyone an' that.

DUMMEY: Does Laura know?

SHELLEY: She telt me. (*beat*) Do you like Mick and Sylv then?

DUMMEY: Aye they're class. I thought Mick was gonna be scary but he was nice.

SHELLEY: You proper perked him up.

DUMMEY: He talks dead weird doesn't he?

SHELLEY: Ees from laandan. They do talk weird down there.

DUMMEY: I didn't understand everything he said. What's the Michael thing? Who is he?

SHELLEY: Ees Mick's son. The' caal him Michael Jr. See him on the photies behind you?

DUMMEY: This smiling one? Ee does look like 'is.

She starts to go.

DUMMEY: Shelley. How erm. I mean. Can I? When d'yous all?

SHELLEY: You'll be comin' in the afternoons. Just after school. Divin't wait around outsidee. Just walk in to the porch. Knock once. Wait for the yes. It's never locked. (*beat*) And don't bring anyone. That's important.

DUMMEY: OK.

SHELLEY: I mean it Dummey. Don't bring anyone.

SCENE 2

DEAN is standing centre stage, PYTHON in hand, looming large. Knock at the door.

DUMMEY: (*O.S.*) Hello? Mick?

DUMMEY enters.

DEAN: Fuck off.

Beat. DUMMEY Frozen.

DUMMEY: Sorry. (*DEAN is suddenly over him*) I. I divin't want any trouble.

DEAN: Fuck off then.

DUMMEY: It's the afternoon.

DEAN: (*Gently*) You're not welcome. What've you heard aboot this place?

DUMMEY frozen.

DEAN: Ye wanna be careful/ coming.

MICK enters through the main door with shopping bags. He salutes DUMMEY. Ignoring DEAN, he moves straight through. DEAN begins putting the snake back.

MICK: /There he is! Alright bonny boy! I was hoping we'd see you again. (*To CLARK in the KITCHEN*) Lieutenant Gable! There he is. Guess who's here lad? Yes, he is.

SYLV enters with shopping bags. Initially to DEAN;

SYLV: Hello pet.

DUMMEY looks at DEAN.

SYLV: What? What's going on? Dean?

MICK re-enters.

MICK: 'Ttension. If you'll pardon the pun.

DUMMEY: I've gotta go.

MICK: (*grabs DUMMEY*) Don't go yet.

DEAN looks at MICK and snorts.

MICK: You not got somewhere to be?

DEAN moves towards the door.

SYLV: (*SYLV hands MICK bags*) Take these. Dean pet. Hoy. Grumpelstiltskin.

DEAN: What man?

SYLV: Don't spend yer money down the Feathers pet.

MICK: (*O.S.*) TORY pub. Terrible beer.

SYLV: We've got plenty of/ drink for yous...

/He exits.

SYLV: (*of DEAN*) What's got into him?

MICK: (*to DUMMEY*) You better pay your respects to Clark. He's all excited now.

MICK ushers DUMMEY into taking his shoes off neatly and going to the KITCHEN to see CLARK. SYLV twitches the curtains. MICK returns.

MICK:	(*of DEAN*) Teenage angst.
SYLV:	He's in his twenties.
MICK:	He ignores *me* all the ruddy time.
SYLV:	(*quietly*) Not keen on the bairn.
MICK:	Dummey?
SYLV:	Shush man.
MICK:	They've only just met!
SYLV:	Y'know he said the most horrible, thing the other day. Racist.
MICK:	That's the modern world Sylv. Indi-ruddyvidualism. Disenfranchised youth lashing out at/
SYLV:	/We're losin' him.
MICK:	Good. Stop him hanging round here like a bad rash.
SYLV:	It's you he's angry at man. Make an effort.
	(*DUMMEY re-enters*) Please?
	(*to DUMMEY*) Flower, did Dean allow you in?
MICK:	Leave the lad alone will you?
SYLV:	You knocked?
DUMMEY:	Like Shelley said to.
SYLV:	And Dean allowed you in, that was it?

MICK: (In a Euro accent) Ja mein captor zat iz all! (*kissing her, she says OK*)

SYLV takes the shopping back off MICK and exits to KITCHEN. MICK picks up a paper, covered in news on the invasion of Iraq. MICK sits and pats the chair next to him.

Beat as DUMMEY hesitates, then sits.

DUMMEY: (*quietly*) Why've yous got all that Viking stuff?

MICK: Eh?

DUMMEY: Helmets an' that?

MICK: Oh. Me and Sylv are Norse warriors.

DUMMEY: You're a warrior?

MICK: On a Sunday. Just round the house. (*Viking voice*) Me Stigander, it mean wanderer. I pillage. I wander. I kill.

DUMMEY laughs as MICK grunts and acts like a Viking. SYLV enters putting away some fruit in the dining room.

MICK: Ah! She IMPI, it mean Virgin.

SYLV: Of all things.

MICK: (*still as the Viking*) It ruddy misleading

SYLV: Good actress y'see?

DUMMEY: Does Dean do it?

MICK: Dean couldn't imagine his lunch mate, let alone be a Viking warrior.

SYLV:	Why d'you ask?
MICK:	Isn't time you were at church you great sinner?
SYLV:	(*looking at the clock*) Ee fuck a duck. You're right.
DUMMEY:	You go to church?
SYLV:	(*grabbing stuff together*) What you trying to say like? Could I not be a nice little old lady?
DUMMEY:	Erm.
SYLV:	Yer silence is deafenin'.
MICK:	He doesn't think a sexual predator like you could be a God botherer.

DUMMEY laughs.

SYLV:	Why d'you think I go man?
MICK:	Sinner through and through.
SYLV:	I'll be sinning with you when I get back, on the proviso that you two behave.
MICK:	What kind of sinning per chance?
SYLV:	Dealer's choice. Right see you later lover boy. And you Mickey.

She kisses MICK, squeezes his crotch.

MICK:	(*to DUMMEY*) Ooh that smarts.

SYLV whispers to MICK 'find out etc'. She exits.

42

DUMMEY: See you.

Beat

MICK: Man time it is. And while we're on the subject. Ever made a crossbow?

DUMMEY: I don't think so.

MICK: D'you wanna?

DUMMEY: Aye.

MICK: Got any string?

DUMMEY: Me Mam has.

MICK: You bring the string, we'll make a crossbow.

DUMMEY: OK.

He sits right next to DUMMEY.

MICK: What did he really say then?

DUMMEY: What?

MICK: It's OK, I won't be annoyed.

DUMMEY: Erm.

MICK: Dean's with us. That means he's with you. Ruddy useful lad to know an' all.

DUMMEY: Does he... protect you?

MICK: We protect him more like.

DUMMEY: Does he live here?

MICK:	May as ruddy well do. Not that we get a pennies rent. He's like Tory porn that kid. A work shy, benefit scrounging, council estate, danger to the community. He's an Ian Duncan Smith wet dream.
DUMMEY:	Why's he here?
MICK:	Good question! He's part of the ruddy furniture. Come on. Would you rather screw in a nice warm bed or at the ressy?
DUMMEY:	Anywhere for me.

MICK laughs.

DUMMEY:	Who's he... Shaggin'?
MICK:	Her upstairs. Literally. Louisa. You won't see 'er. She's like a ruddy ninja.
DUMMEY:	They just stay up there?
MICK:	Would you rather im' out there, terrorising the bus stop?
DUMMEY:	You don't mind them doing it?
MICK:	Natural isn't it.

MICK picks up two remote controls. He switches the TV on. "Iraq making fresh efforts to cooperate with the UN". MICK uses the remote with ineptitude, he changes channel and the soft porn film is still playing.

| MICK: | Now this is what I call Man time. |

DUMMEY smiles and nods enthusiastically.

MICK:	Was it about me was it? What he said? I'm 'is favourite subject.

Beat. No answer.

MICK:	In the words of Sweden's finest... Does your Mother know that you're out?
DUMMEY:	What?
MICK:	Does she know you're here?
DUMMEY:	Should I tell her?
MICK:	Well that's up to you. Is it a good idea?
DUMMEY:	Erm.
MICK:	She'd stop you comin?
DUMMEY:	Nah. I mean she might kick off a bit but...
MICK:	But? Yer old man?
DUMMEY:	Kev. I don't think he'd like you.
MICK:	That's charming that lad.
DUMMEY:	No I.
MICK:	(*playfully pokes DUMMEY*) Cos I was thinking. You could probably walk Clark tomorrow afternoon? If you were comin' back o' course?
DUMMEY:	I could walk him mesel'?
MICK:	Well I'll have to check with the boss. (*Indicates Clark, pretends to bark conversation*) Yep he says he's alright.

45

DUMMEY: Maybes I shouldn't tell them the whole truth.

MICK: Spoken like a true Blairite.

DUMMEY: I might say I'm at football.

MICK: You say whatever you need to, to come and see old Mick.

DUMMEY: Shelley said I should come in the afternoons?

MICK: Word of advice on rules. When you're breaking 'em.

DUMMEY: Yeah?

MICK: Don't get caught.

MICK winks, pats DUMMEY's face. They are physically close. DUMMEY notices something in the porn and they both laugh/gasp. DEAN enters, quietly through the front door.

Stops, watches MICK and DUMMEY. MICK feels his presence. Sitting up MICK turns the porn off.

MICK: Ruddy hell the second comin'? What you playin' at shuffling in? You'll give 'is a ruddy heart attack.

DEAN continues in to the snake.

MICK: 'Hello Mick, how are you? I'm fine thanks Dean, yourself?'

DEAN ignores MICK. DUMMEY straining to look as DEAN takes a mouse from the fridge.

MICK: Can the boy come and have a look?

DUMMEY: I don't wanna disturb her.

MICK: Go on. Meet Vivian Leigh. (*DUMMEY approaches*) Show 'im 'ow to feed her then.

DEAN: She isn't feeding. She's sick.

Impasse. MICK stares DEAN down. DEAN moves aside, invites DUMMEY in.

DUMMEY: (*to DEAN*) Can I stroke her?

MICK: Can you stroke the snake? There's an offer eh Dean?

DUMMEY: I just wanna touch her.

MICK: Cor it's like carry on cobra in 'ere today.

DEAN loses patience. DEAN suddenly picks up DUMMEY, allowing DUMMEY the height to reach into the tank and, with caution, stroke the snake.

DUMMEY: (*of the snake*) Cold.

DEAN nods. Puts him down.

DUMMEY: (*looking at DEAN properly for the first time*) You not gonna feed her?

DEAN: She doesn't need it.

Seals up the tank.

MICK: Didn't fancy the delights of Costa Del Bus stop today then Deano? Nice can of ignorance wif the lads down the Feathers?

DEAN rejects this mumbling, skulks back upstairs.

MICK:	Oh, come on man it's a joke. Thank you for the hospitality Mick, Thanks for the warm bed. Ungrateful shit.
	(*to DUMMEY*) I tell you, I wish he'd shut up that lad. Giving it all this (*he mimes chatty sign*).
DUMMEY:	He is quiet, isn't he?
MICK:	Quiet? There's more noise in a ruddy vacuum.
DUMMEY:	I hate that noise. Does he ever speak?
MICK:	He always used to. Sylv still gets him going occasionally. Right ruddy pair of conspirators those two are. Ruddy soft on him.
DUMMEY:	Why would you have a tattoo on yer face?
MICK:	Good question! Can ye imagine them at down at Geordie Scott's? Anchor sir? Mermaid on the arm perhaps? Nah I'll have the big blue tear on me cheek thanks. Probably a metaphor.
DUMMEY:	It's crazy whatever it is.
MICK:	There were loads of 'em, before. Brothers. Four of 'em I think. Imagine that! All with those tears.
DUMMEY:	What happened to the other three?
MICK:	Accountants. (*beat. Smiles. Then distant*) Nah. They're erm AWOL. Gone.
DUMMEY:	They're where?

MICK: Mind you he's not quiet when he gets upstairs. Like a ruddy zoo those two. Who's gonna tell him off? Not me. (*pulls a face like Dean's*) Scary.

DUMMEY laughs.

DUMMEY: I don't think he heard 'is knock.

MICK deliberately silent

DEAN: And. He said. When I came in. He says. 'I wanna be careful?'

MICK: You wanna be careful? What here? (*beat*) Well careful's right, don't want you walking in on me willy-nilly. Got to have some rules y'know. Careful it is. I'll speak to him about careful don't you fret.

DUMMEY: Is it OK if I come back?

MICK: Do ye wanna?

DUMMEY: Um.

MICK: I want you to.

DUMMEY: Really?

MICK: Yeah. So there! And I want you out of that ruddy shell o' yours an' all...

DUMMEY: Ok.

MICK: Good boy. You're gonna like it here son. (*MICK strokes DUMMEY'S head*) You're gonna love it.

SCENE 3

EARLY MORNING.

SHELLEY watching Hans Blix and Iraq news. DUMMEY knocks once.

SHELLEY: You're late.

DUMMEY pokes his head in.

DUMMEY: It's the middle of the night.

SHELLEY: It's 7.03.

DUMMEY: That's the middle of the night. Where's Mick and Sylv?

SHELLEY: (*retrieving a piece of paper from her pocket; reads*) The Formulae 1 hotel. Ponteland Airport.

DUMMEY: Are the' racing? Are the' flying?

SHELLEY: What are ye like the transport police?

DUMMEY: Just tell 'is!

SHELLEY: It's Valentine's.

DUMMEY: Oh.

SHELLEY: They'll be back in a bit. Mick'll never stay actual Valentine's day, cos he says he won't be seen to buy into 'the mass ruddy commercialisation of love enforced by the ruddy corporations'.

Beat

DUMMEY: Why are we here?

SHELLEY: You've told people.

DUMMEY: What?

SHELLEY: You've told someone at school.

DUMMEY: No!

SHELLEY: Don't lie.

DUMMEY: I'm not lying.

SHELLEY: Good.

Beat

DUMMEY: Is that it?

SHELLEY: It was on me mind.

DUMMEY: Could you not've asked 'is this at school?

SHELLEY: We never talk at school.

DUMMEY: We never talk at seven in the morning!

SHELLEY: Did anyone see you leave?

DUMMEY: Nee-one else is awake!

SHELLEY: What've ye telt your Dad?

DUMMEY: Kev. Football training.

SHELLEY: *You* playing football?

DUMMEY: Shut up.

SHELLEY: Well don't say anything to anyone.

DUMMEY: OK! God. Where's all this come from?

SHELLEY: We need to trust you.

DUMMEY: Why don't we say owt to anyone? Does Sylv say not to?

SHELLEY: No.

DUMMEY: Are Mick and Sylv. Weird?

SHELLEY: I Dunno. Laura'll says she'll be over tonight. If you are.

DUMMEY: Oh?

SHELLEY: She says if you come she'll wear a Pencil skirt.

DUMMEY: I might, might not. What's a pencil skirt?

SHELLEY: It's got a slit.

Beat. DUMMEY gulps.

DUMMEY: Why did you think something was wrong?

SHELLEY: I didn't, Dean did.

DUMMEY: What did Dean say?

SHELLEY: You think he doesn't like you. You're right.

DUMMEY: Don't care.

Beat. SHELLEY watches TV. DUMMEY finds his way to the snake.

SHELLEY: Dean'll go fuckin' mental if you touch Vivian Leigh.

DUMMEY: Is he here?

SHELLEY: Do ye really wanna piss him off?

DUMMEY: Doesn't like 'is anyway so.

DUMMEY looks in the tank. Slides back the lid of the tank.

DUMMEY: What do I do?

SHELLEY: Ask Dean.

DUMMEY frowns. Looking away from the open tank, he opens the fridge and retrieves a frozen mouse.

DUMMEY: Do I just drop it in?

SHELLEY: I'm tellin' you this isn't a good idea.

DUMMEY: Ah man relax. (*holds the mouse above the tank*) Vivian? It's Breakfast time.

SHELLEY: Do you think she knas what breakfast means?

DUMMEY: It's food time.

SHELLEY: Aye food time'll make more sense. Ye kna she doesn't have ears.

DUMMEY: Do they not?

SHELLEY: Just drop it in before anyone comes.

DUMMEY: I can't see her.

SHELLEY: She'll be asleep, her head'll be in the Pink castle, just drop it.

DUMMEY: Shelley, I don't think she's in.

SHELLEY: She's not popped to the hair dressers.

DUMMEY: Honestly, I think she's out.

SHELLEY: Out? Dummey man, she doesn't dee the school run.

DUMMEY: Here you wanna come over and have a look at this like. Honestly, she's not in the pink castle, or in the moat or the helmet /

SHELLEY: (*sighs – annoyed*) God. (*looking in*) Shit where's the snake!

DUMMEY: What? Where is she?

SHELLEY: She's a Six-foot python Dummey. You notice when she's not there. Fuck!

DUMMEY: Fuck Dean's gonna kill 'is.

SHELLEY: It's the python that'll kill wer.

DUMMEY: Shit! (*he jumps on the couch*) What do we do?

SHELLEY: Find it!

DUMMEY: (*wipes sweat from his face. Screams*) Ah!

DUMMEY throws something across the room towards Shelley.

SHELLEY: What ye deein?

DUMMEY: I just rubbed me face with a frozen mouse.

SHELLEY: What you deein' that for?

DUMMEY: I forgot I was holdin' it.

SHELLEY: Well don't throw it at me!

DUMMEY: I wasn't aiming for you!

SHELLEY: What you doing on the settee?

DUMMEY: There's a python loose!

SHELLEY: They live in trees in the woods, I don't think she'll have much bother with the three-piece suite.

DUMMEY: Ah shit. (*he looks under his feet and above his head*) Ah God. Vivian?

SHELLEY: The' don't have ears.

DUMMEY: Vivian Leigh?

SHELLEY: Using her full name won't help then!

DUMMEY: I was thinkin' she might get confused and think we're after someone else.

SHELLEY: SHE'S A SNAKE MAN.

DUMMEY: I'm scared. Are you?

SHELLEY: No.

DUMMEY: Nah. Me neither. What do we do if we find her?

SHELLEY: Put her back in her tank.

DUMMEY: You mean pick her up?

SHELLEY: What's your plan like? Ask her politely? You're the one obsessed with feeding her.

DUMMEY: That was before I knew I was gonna pick her up.

SHELLEY: She must have jumped out. Here get up the dresser and have a look.

DUMMEY: No way

SHELLEY: You lost her.

DUMMEY: I can't.

SHELLEY: Howeh I'll give ye a bunk.

DUMMEY: What if she bites 'is on the face?

SHELLEY: It'll improve you.

DUMMEY: (*beat. Gets on*) Oh God. Where am I looking?

SHELLEY: Top shelf.

DUMMEY: Push 'is then. Higher. Slowly.

SHELLEY: You're too short.

DUMMEY: Fuck off! You're too heavy.

SHELLEY: Fuck off.

MICK and SYLV enter.

DUMMEY: Can you get your hand under me leg?

SHELLEY: Your cock's rubbing me chin.

DUMMEY: It's an accident obviously. Can you get me arse on your head?

SHELLEY: Spread your legs then.

DUMMEY: Push 'is further in then.

DUMMEY and SHELLEY in an uncompromising position.

MICK: Ruddy hell.

Kids remain. Frozen to the spot.

SYLV:	I've done some extreme positions in my time, but this.
MICK:	We've only been away a night. When did you lot turn into Zippo's ruddy sex Circus?

They turn around.

SHELLEY:	(*light*) Alright Sylv.
DUMMEY:	(*breezy*) Morning.
SYLV:	What the hell are you up to?
SHELLEY:	Nothin'.
DUMMEY:	Nothin'.
MICK:	Nothin'?
DUMMEY:	Stretching?
SYLV:	(*in DUMMEY's face*) If you don't tell me what's going on, in two seconds flat /
SHELLEY:	/ Dummey opened the case, even though I told him not to /
DUMMEY:	/ Shelley man! /
SHELLEY:	/ He wanted to feed her a mouse but he threw the mouse away.
DUMMEY:	I forgot I was holding it!
SHELLEY:	It was all him.
DUMMEY:	Shut up Shelley!
SHELLEY:	I was watching GMTV.

DUMMEY: She was distracting 'is.

SYLV and MICK have clocked what's happened.

MICK: What exactly 'ave you done?

DUMMEY: Promise you won't stop 'is coming?

SYLV: Depends on what it is you done, doesn't it love?

MICK: Yes Sylv. Depends on what you've done son. I'd come clean if I were you.

SYLV: Wouldn't want to force it out of you.

Beat.

DUMMEY: I lost Vivian Leigh.

Keeping a straight face.

SYLV: You lost a six-foot python?

MICK: What the ruddy hell were you doing to lose a snake?

SYLV: You know what it's like Mickey. You put your six-foot python down for one minute.

DUMMEY: I wanted to feed her.

SYLV: Dean said she wasn't well.

SHELLEY: She jumped out the case.

MICK: Jumped? Like a jump?

He jumps with two legs.

DUMMEY: We think she's on the dresser.

SYLV:	Where's Dean?
SHELLEY:	He didn't stay over.
SYLV:	He didn't stay in an empty house? (*suspicious*) Who did?
SHELLEY:	Just me.
SYLV:	Where is he now?
SHELLEY:	On top of the dresser.
SYLV:	Dean.
SHELLEY:	He went down the town last night. He didn't come back.

Beat. MICK arm on the top of the dresser.

MICK:	Reconnaissance! That's what's needed here. Private Dummett reconnoitre the bathroom and pay particular attention to the toilet bowl. Cleaning as you go. Lance Corporal inspect and tidy every inch of our bedroom. This is life and death you two. Code red. Find our snake.

They hurry upstairs. Beat.

MICK:	Did you see their little faces!
SYLV:	He looked like he'd shat himself!
MICK:	Young Shel' was white as a ruddy sheet. When are you going to let on?
SYLV:	I reckon we can stretch it out. Until she's back from the vets.

MICK: Let 'em sweat.

SYLV: Might even get the kitchen cleaned!

Beat.

MICK: What?

SYLV: Nothing.

MICK: What is it?

SYLV: He didn't stay in an empty house. Lord knows where he did stay.

MICK: The same place he stays every other ruddy night. Holiday park? Some ruddy drug addled bloody flat.

SYLV: You think that's OK?

MICK: I think you're OK.

Holds her.

SYLV: Dean's hearin' filth every day. In ees ear. Chat chat chat chat chat.

MICK grabs her and kisses her passionately.

SYLV: About you. About us. (*MICK still kissing her*) What if he listens?

MICK: Good! (*kissing her*)

SYLV: You can't just distract me.

MICK: Can't I?

SYLV: NO. (*MICK playfully kissing her body*)
Maybe.

They laugh. She hauls him up.

MICK: Dean's not leavin'. My soldiers never desert.

Kisses her, she pulls back. Knock at the door.

MICK: (*to door*) NO!

SYLV: Dean?

Kisses her. Letter through the door.

SYLV: What's got into you?

MICK: Apart from you?

They kiss.

MICK: I'm back to my best.

Scene change – perhaps a narrative of MICK reading the letter, hate mail, that's dropped through the door. SYLV tries to see it, he hides it, rips it up.

SCENE 4

MICK stands with a bottle of Tequila containing a worm. The gang surround him, sat at his feet. SYLV on her chair. There is a framed picture, formally on the wall, now leaning against the cabinet.

DUMMEY: Is it real?

SHELLEY: It's so not real.

LAURA: (*grabs DUMMEY*) Ooh! It scares me!

SYLV: I think he's a bit pickled to be scary.

MICK: 40 years ago, in a factory on the isle of Canary, a teeny, tiny worm crawled into an open bottle /

SYLV: / I kna the feeling.

MICK: The factory thought it ruined, so they chucked it out. Into the open ocean. Unwanted. A reject.

SHELLEY: I kna the feeling.

MICK: Well didn't she float on the waves. All the way along the African coast, past, erm, past, you know, the next bit.

SYLV: Portugal /

MICK: / Portugal, precisely, all the way, finally resting... on the glorious North-East coast. Where Clark Gable, found it, buried under a johnny. A natural phenomenomenon. You have a closer look Alan.

62

DUMMEY: It's amazing.

MICK: Who's trying it then?

LAURA: It's full of worm poo.

MICK: Don't be so. Worm poo? Alan?

DUMMEY: Aye. I'm not scared.

DUMMEY takes the bottle and sips a tiny amount from the top of the bottle.

DUMMEY: (*his face twists up in anguish*) Aye. It's really good. Aye.

MICK: (*laughs. Pats DUMMEY's cheek*) That's my boy.

SYLV: Whey we should dee it properly.

MICK: Good thinking Batwoman. Les fetch the lemon and salt.

She does.

MICK: This is the way to drink it son. We've had a few o' ruddy these in our time eh Sylvie?

SYLV: The only time I've seen a human being go from sitting down, on four legs, vertical, to completely horizontal.

DUMMEY: Who?

SYLV: Him man!

DUMMEY: (*laughing*) Did ye Mick?

SHELLEY: Thought you had guts o' steel?

MICK: I do! I do! It was the prawns!

SYLV: Oh, not the bloody prawns again.

MICK: A bad prawn can make you very ruddy
                   unstable.

SYLV: (*laughing*) I'm tellin' ye man. He was like this.
                   (*she shows them*) The next second, he was like
                   this!

SHELLEY back with bits.

SHELLEY: Yous only had a satsuma and Canderel.

MICK: That'll do. That'll do. Right son, have
                   another sip.

DUMMEY: How d'you do it?

MICK: So, put the Canderel, between your teeth, like
                   so.

He does. SYLV peels the orange. Eats some.

SYLV: Drink a shot and then bite into this.

MICK: Right... on three.

DUMMEY: I've swallowed the Canderel by accident.

MICK: Three!

*He drinks. DUMMEY eats the orange and coughs and spurts.
Ha. That's the ruddy spirit. Put hairs on that naked chest o' yours.*

LAURA: (*to DUMMEY*) I love a bare chest. I
                   wouldn't want all that hair in your face.

SYLV: (*withering – to SHELLEY*) So full of mystery, isn't she?

MICK offers LAURA the bottle.

SHELLEY: (*of the bottle*) Here I'll look after that. (*drinks throughout*)

SYLV: Aye, I don't think the Canderel method'll catch on.

MICK: Come on then Yoof. Don't hold back. It's art attack time.

MICK turns the picture around revealing a backboard of names. The kids dive towards the picture. MICK grabs pens. The names DEAN, LOUISA, LAURA and SHELLEY stick out. Graffiti type fonts. With height lines etc on the reverse of the frame.

MICK: Now. Master Dummett, as the youngest, newest, second most handsome member of the household, I think, this year, you should be first.

DUMMEY: What do I write?

MICK: Well, just write your name or something you'll remember in a few years.

DUMMEY: I'm gonna draw I think.

MICK: Oh right.

SYLV: Don't you dare. My girls wait on no man.

The GIRLS begin. DUMMEY begins drawing, tongue out.

SHELLEY: I'm writing, Laura loves Dummey, if destroyed still true forever.

LAURA: (*genuinely embarrassed*) Shelley man! I'm writing Shelley loves Mick.

SYLV: She can keep her hands off. That sagging arse's all mine!

MICK: Oi!

She slaps it. They laugh. DEAN enters and hangs back, he smiles, watching.

LAURA: Look at Dean's graphs. They're class.

SYLV: (*aware he's there*) He's a talented boy when he wants to be.

DUMMEY: This is class this like.

SHELLEY: There's so many names. Yous'll have to replace the back.

MICK: Replace the? Hear that Sylv? There's your throw away consumer culture. Everything must ruddy go.

SHELLEY: I cannot even remember most o' these.

SYLV: Aye we've had a few through the door.

DEAN approaches the group with a pen.

MICK: (*Turning to DEAN, protecting DUMMEY's spot*) A few too many I think.

SYLV catches this as DEAN shuffles upstairs.

SYLV: (*Shouting after him*) Oh, Dean pet? You need to write your name.

SHELLEY:	Here Lau have seen your height line from last year. You've gone down I think.
MICK:	What we feeding these girls?
LAURA:	(*distressed*) I'm not that short.
SYLV:	Divin't fret look at him.
MICK:	Good things come in small packages eh Sylvie my love?
SYLV:	Aye lucky for you.
LAURA:	Hardly lucky for me though. It makes 'is look fat.
SYLV:	You?
LAURA:	Look here! Someone's drawn 'is here dead fat.
SYLV:	That's a stick-man.
LAURA:	More like a log-man.
SYLV:	How can a stick-man be fat?
LAURA:	This one is! She's got fat arms.
SYLV:	They've just used a felt tip man.
LAURA:	Aye cos my arms are fat.
SHELLEY:	Her face is the same colour as the wall man.
SYLV:	It's not a life drawing.
LAURA:	Why've I got a massive green cock?
SYLV:	Let me see. (*of MICK*) That's him. It's not even you.

67

LAURA:	That means that I'm that'un. That's even worse. She's minging.
SHELLEY:	Minging?
MICK:	You see that Sylvie. This is exactly it. Whoring the unrealistic capitalist lie of Materialism and male affirmation to our young girls. Sex in the ruddy City? What d'you ruddy expect?
LAURA:	Oh, I love Sex and the City though.
SHELLEY:	Aye it's funny that show like.
SYLV:	Out voted!
MICK:	You think our Laura's perfect don't you son?
LAURA:	D' you Dummey?
DUMMEY:	Erm, yeah.
SYLV:	Talk about unrealistic representation. Look at the size of your green cock.
MICK:	You've never complained about the colour before.
SYLV:	If anyone ever tells you that size doesn't matter girls, they're lying. It absolutely does.
LAURA:	Am I too short?
DUMMEY:	I think you're a really nice height.
LAURA:	Do you?
SYLV:	(*looking at the picture*) How you getting on Picasso?

68

DUMMEY:	Nearly done.
SHELLEY:	What is it?
DUMMEY:	Done.
LAURA:	I know what it is.
SYLV:	(*reading, glasses on. Cold*) Me and Mick Porsche time. Besties.
MICK:	Ah. That's lovely that Alan.
LAURA:	So lush.
MICK:	(*strokes DUMMEY's hair*) Thank you, my boy. Eh Sylv?
SYLV:	Hmm.

The sound of DEAN and LOUISA starting again from upstairs.

SHELLEY:	Here we go.
MICK:	Warming the place up for us eh?
SYLV:	I've just changed the sheets.
LAURA:	(*to DUMMEY*) I like it. The noise.
SHELLEY:	(*coughs*) Desperate.
DUMMEY:	Can we go out in the Porsche soon Mick?
MICK:	I'm sure that could be arranged.
DUMMEY:	Yes.
MICK:	Fastest Porsche in the North East.

69

SYLV: (*sharp*) I thought you were collecting wer dinners at 5?

MICK: You take Shelley, I'll see to the 'yoof'.

SYLV: I'll see the bairns out. Go on. Dinner time.

MICK: I promised the boy I'd show him something.

SYLV stares at MICK, she won't be beaten in public.

SYLV: Are you eating Shelley?

SHELLEY: Aye.

SYLV: It's just from the fishy mind.

LAURA: Be a massive queue on valentines.

SHELLEY: I'll come with you and wait.

SYLV: You'll have to stay in the car.

LAURA: Can we eat here Sylv?

SYLV: No.

LAURA: Shelley is.

SYLV: You know why she stays Laura. You know why you don't. Howay mes enfant. Move.

MICK: They haven't got their shoes on.

SYLV: Two minutes.

MICK grabs DUMMEY and LAURA just as SYLV leaves.

MICK: Hang about you two.

SHELLEY looks to MICK.

SHELLEY: Sylv said they couldn't stay.

MICK: Oh, come on Corp'. Bit of rope?

SHELLEY: I'm not lying to Sylv.

MICK: Did I ask you to lie?

SHELLEY: Nah you asked 'is for rope.

MICK: Just let her know they were on their merry way eh?

SHELLEY unsure.

LAURA: I covered for you when you drank Sylv's vodka.

MICK: Leverage.

SHELLEY puts her shoes on. LAURA hurries over to DUMMEY.

LAURA: It's a bit dark outside. I'll be scared walking home alone now.

SHELLEY: (*to herself*) Oh my God.

LAURA: It's just, dressed like this. I think I'm getting palpitations.

SHELLEY: You have no self-respect.

DUMMEY: I'll walk you if you like? After Mick's thing?

SHELLEY groans. Exits after SYLV.

LAURA: Would you?

MICK: What you two need is a place to keep each other warm. Eh Alan?

DUMMEY: What we stayin' for Mick?

MICK: Ah ha!

MICK dashes out to the kitchen leaving DUMMEY and LAURA alone. Awkward pause. Both are socially awkward and shy.

DUMMEY: So erm you got school on Monday?

LAURA: Yeah.

DUMMEY: Yeah. Me too.

Beat. MICK returns, humming and singing 'One Corneto', with a can of cheap lager, two glasses, a tea towel, and an ash tray. He places them on an occasional table and ushers DUMMEY and LAURA to sit next to each other. He plays Kate Bush's 'Wurthering Heights'.

MICK: Mooood music.

DUMMEY and LAURA laugh awkwardly.

MICK: Now don't mind me. I'm invisible. I'm not here.

MICK goes to the kitchen. Quiet CLARK sounds. Beat.

DUMMEY: (*he can't open the can*) I bite me nails too much.

LAURA: I'll do it.

She does.

DUMMEY: I really like your skirt.

LAURA:	Do you?
DUMMEY:	Good slit.
LAURA:	What?
DUMMEY:	The skirt.
LAURA:	Oh.
DUMMEY:	You look really like good looking and that.
LAURA:	(*changing her hair*) No, I don't.

MICK bursts in with a tea towel on his head, feeling his way blindly to a lighter and cigarettes.

MICK:	Don't mind me. I'm invisible, I'm not here.

They laugh. MICK exits, gives DUMMEY the thumbs up.

DUMMEY:	Nah you do. Like. Really fit.
LAURA:	Do I?
DUMMEY:	And really nice.
LAURA:	Shut up man.
DUMMEY:	Your hair's long.
LAURA:	You're a proper gentleman.
DUMMEY:	Can I get off with you?
LAURA:	Aye. If you want to. Wait. Have you got any chud?
DUMMEY:	Oh. Aye.

He fishes around in his pocket for the chewing gum.

DUMMEY: Shit. I've only got one bit.

LAURA: Give us it. I'll pass it to you.

DUMMEY: OK.

He makes a tiny move towards her.

LAURA: Come here then.

They awkwardly embrace. They lean in for the kiss slowly.

LAURA: You can feel my tit if you want.

SCENE 5

MICK is in the LIVING ROOM sweeping up broken glass.
DUMMEY enters. There is a piece of cardboard on the window.
DUMMEY immediately takes his shoes off and places them
neatly.

MICK: Afternoon son. Didn't think I'd see you on a weekend?

DUMMEY: Should I go? (*they smile*) What y' doin?

MICK: Oh, some little ruddy rapscallions chucked this through. (*he shows DUMMEY half a BRICK*) Thought I'd clean it up before Slvie sees it.

DUMMEY: Did anyone get hurt?

MICK: (*smiles*) Tea?

DUMMEY: Aye it'll need a bag in the mug. And some milk. And stirring.

MICK: Is that right? (*MICK tickles his ribs*) I'm the mug makin' you a brew every day this week.

DUMMEY: (*while he's tickled, he's shrieking almost, fighting to get the words out*) I cannot do it. I'm pagga'd. You're just lazy.

MICK: Little monkey. Ha. (*as he exits*) What's Pagga'd when it's at home? Bloomin' Geordie nonsense. (*as he's exiting*) I'll learn ya to talk proper.

DUMMEY feeds the snake. Jumps on the couch, relaxed. The
TV is showing the march against the war.

DUMMEY: (*shouting through*) Mick. Do you think we should bomb the Middle East?

MICK: (*O.S.*) I'm making you tea I can't do everything all at once.

DUMMEY: Nah I mean because of these 9/11 ragheads an' that. Do you think we should just drop one on the lot of them?

MICK: (*back in the room*) I beg your pardon?

DUMMEY: Saddam's violated conventions and ees had Al-Queda round for a cup of tea. Payback time.

MICK: Which convention would that be? The violated one?

DUMMEY: Eh?

MICK: (*smiling*) You don't know what that is do you?

DUMMEY: Yes, I do.

MICK: Get outta here. (*turns back to KITCHEN*)

DUMMEY: I've never known what I wanted to do.

MICK: (*still light hearted*) Well this is quite a jump!

DUMMEY: Mick! Listen! I wanna go and fight like you.

MICK: I don't wanna fight.

DUMMEY: But.

MICK: Now don't get me ruddy wrong. I respect them lads. Unimaginable ruddy job that.

DUMMEY:	So why can't I do it?
MICK:	Cos it's not what needs fightin' son. (*picks up the brick?*) Fear. Ignorance. Discontent.
DUMMEY:	I've already signed up for sea cadets. I can do what you did.
MICK:	No son you can't.
DUMMEY:	Scared I'll do better than you?
MICK:	Scared yes.
DUMMEY:	Aye well I wanna protect people. Me Mam, Laura.
MICK:	From who?
DUMMEY:	Ragheeds / next door!
MICK:	Oi!
DUMMEY:	We've opened the floodgates and now they're running the shop.

Beat. MICK is surprised by DUMMEY.

MICK:	That's enough. Son. You're not to say that/
DUMMEY:	No Middle East. No problem.
MICK:	You could say that about us. (*checks himself*) Why am I arguing?
DUMMEY:	So, you're allowed but I'm not? I'm not scared of danger.
MICK:	It's your fear that's fuckin' dangerous. A war on ruddy 'Terror', it's unending. There's no

stoppin' terror. That's why they've shortened the ruddy word! / Son.

DUMMEY: What if they bomb Newcastle?

MICK: With what?

DUMMEY: Better them than us/ I.

MICK: You ever had to deal with grief?

DUMMEY: Yeah.

MICK: Not your fuckin' Gran or your guinea pig. I'm talking about death.

DUMMEY: I have.

MICK: You wouldn't know death if he hit you in the face.

DUMMEY: I would.

MICK: Always the same, cowards, who'd shit themselves on the front. Screaming for blood from the back!

DUMMEY: I'd be right at the front!

MICK: Front of what? You gonna punish them are ya? Gonna hurt somebody?

DUMMEY: I'm not the one who's been to war.

MICK: Exactly why / you should listen.

DUMMEY: / And you've been to prison.

MICK: And do you know what it's like? What it's really fucking like? To Kill? To lose? It hurts.

You wanna see cripples and bodies to prove you're a man?

DUMMEY: You cannit stop 'is protectin' me family.

MICK: I ruddy well am. You'll stay right here in this house.

DUMMEY: You can't stop 'is leavin'.

He walks towards the door. The argument has become quite blurred.

MICK: (*catching him*) No, you do not. Rich men start wars, young men fuckin' die in them.

DUMMEY: Kev says.

MICK: I don't give a monkey's what Kev says. Who the fuck is Kev? /

DUMMEY: / Me.

MICK: (*right at DUMMEY*) / Has Kev seen someone with no limbs? Is that who's feeding you this shit? If he knew. If he could fuckin' imagine. Arsehole. Give 'em a target, feed 'em fear. They'll forget the cockroaches and the dirt under their finger nails, they'll forgive their fuckin' offspring comin' back in a box, as long as it's somebody else's fault. Stick some glitter on a poppy, that should distract the poor bastards from the coffins long enough. (*referencing the T.V.*) Not in my name. Not in my ruddy name? Well as long as it's not in your name and yer feet are tired from all the marchin'. No one does a fuckin' thing.

	Imperialist, Capitalist, religious shite. And you clap them along. Prick.
DUMMEY:	No.
MICK:	Ooh mammy I'm scared, I'm angry, him next door, him at home. KILL THEM ALL! COWARD. War is wrong. Violence is wrong!
DUMMEY:	Alright!
MICK:	Say it. Say it! Say I'm wrong.
DUMMEY:	I'm wrong.
MICK:	I don't know what I'm talking about.
DUMMEY:	I don't know what I'm talking about.
MICK:	No, you fuckin' don't. (*throws something*)

DUMMEY stands stock still, shaken and tearing. MICK walks about a bit, picking things up. He paces into the kitchen, slamming the door. Returns with a glass of water.

DUMMEY:	(*teary*) I have lost.
MICK:	(*going to him*) Son, I'm sorry.
DUMMEY:	I have.

Beat. DUMMEY places his hands on his face tightly.

MICK:	Oh. (*sighing, swearing, improv. DUMMEY won't look at him*) Come on lad. Eh? Al? Mate?
DUMMEY:	(*tears*) You don't know anything.
MICK:	I don't.

DUMMEY: You didn't know him.

MICK: Who? (*slowly realising*) Not your Dad? (*rubbing his face*) Oh, Christ man. Your old man? I didn't know. Christ. Son.

DUMMEY still with hands clamped to his face.

MICK: I shouldn't of / said it. I'm sorry. You were just repeating.

DUMMEY: / I thought you were different.

MICK: I am.

DUMMEY: No, you're not.

MICK: Son I'm as ruddy different as they get. This fella at home ees not your dad?

DUMMEY: Neither are you.

Beat. MICK hurt.

MICK: I'm gonna protect you.

DUMMEY: No.

MICK: Touched a nerve. That's all.

DUMMEY: Cos, I look like Michael? Sylv said. Where is he?

MICK: He wanted to leave.

DUMMEY: Did you not make him stay? Everyone listens to you. (*beat*) He's probably OK, if he's like you. (*beat*) He isn't OK. Is he? (*beat*) But you don't like sayin' it. (*beat*) Me neither.

81

MICK: (*rubbing his face again, beat*) Oh boy. There's no fool like an old fool.

DUMMEY: Sorry.

MICK: C'm 'ere.

MICK, on his knees, hugs DUMMEY. The hug is happily reciprocated. The hug lasts. At that moment DEAN enters via the stairs. He lingers. DEAN stares at the two of them. They break the hug. Kneeling opposite each other.

DUMMEY: I better go home.

MICK nods.

MICK: Problem Dean?

DUMMEY: (*helpfully*) I fed Vivian Leigh.

DEAN: What you lettin' 'im dee that for?

DUMMEY: She needed feedin'.

MICK: Snooze yer ruddy lose eh?

DEAN: (*Turns. Irritated. Bumps into SYLV upon exit*) Fuck's sake man.

MICK: Oooh.

SYLV: Excuse me?

MICK pulls an 'awkward' face. DUMMEY grins.

SYLV: (*to DUMMEY*) What are you doing here? It's a Sunday. (*of DEAN*) What've you said to him?

MICK: Got ees knickers in a ruddy twist.

SYLV: About? (of the brick / window) What's that?

MICK: Accident. My fault.

DUMMEY: We fired a crossbow.

She picks up the brick and the dust pan and goes to the KITCHEN.

SYLV: (*cold, as she goes, to herself*) And yet the brick ended up inside.

MICK: Sharp work Private. How about a reward?

DUMMEY: I've got me dinner.

MICK: Stay over. I'll make you a bed up. Cowboy tea.

DUMMEY: (*surprised*) Stay here? I'll not be allowed.

MICK: Don't mind that. (*sensing it's a no*) What about something else. Err. (*porsche revving sound*)

DUMMEY: (*smiles*) Really? Yes.

He goes. MICK sees him out. Alone. SYLV reenters.

SYLV: Now there's bricks comin' through the windows?

MICK: (*sighing*) 'Kin hell. It's kids.

SYLV: And why are we the target?

Beat.

MICK: (*does a silly SW voice. Forced to trail off*) Cos, we be village weirdos. All them kiddiwinks get guzzled up in this 'ere cave /

She's gone. MICK alone again.

SCENE 6

LAURA alone, waiting for SHELLEY. Banging on the window. She jumps.

LAURA: Dummey?

More banging.

LAURA: Yous can fuck off it's not funny.

The letter box flaps. Opening door.

LAURA: Alright. Jesus.

DEAN: Nar.

LAURA: What you deein?

DEAN says nothing.

LAURA goes back to her seat.

LAURA: You proper shit us up there like.

SYLV: (*O.S.*) Who is it?

DEAN standing in the doorway, says nothing.

LAURA: It's Dean in Sylv.

SYLV: (*O.S.*) Well tell him shut the door.

LAURA: (*shouting*) He is.

DEAN doesn't shut the door.

LAURA: (*sighs gets up*) OK I'll shut the door.

As LAURA goes to the door DEAN blocks LAURA's path. They are close.

85

LAURA:	Ugh. You stink. (*beat*) Louisa's not here. (*hugging herself*) It's freezing.
DEAN:	You're gettin' tapped with the bairn?
LAURA:	So?
DEAN:	It needs to stop.
LAURA:	Why? You jealous?
DEAN:	(*it isn't that but she's touched a nerve*) Shut up man. I'm not jealous of a twelve-year-old kid.
LAURA:	Coulda' fooled me.
DEAN:	It's Mick.
SYLV:	(*O.S.*) Laura I'm trying to do me hair. Why can I feel a draft?
LAURA:	(*looks at DEAN then shouting*) Just havin' a tab out the door Sylv.
DEAN:	If he knew what people're sayin', he wouldn't be hangin' around little kids.
LAURA:	But none of that's true.
DEAN:	You reckon they care?
LAURA:	Who? Yer other friends? So what? They're dicks.
DEAN:	Laura man.
LAURA:	They stuck my head through a winder.
DEAN:	I kna they did.

LAURA: So fuck 'em. It's people like your brothers.
            There's a reason you're the only one left.

DEAN: Cos I'm not like her. I'm better than her.

LAURA: Aye cos of here. Cos of this.

DEAN: You sound like fuckin' Mick.

LAURA: Someone needs to.

DEAN: Yee kna better than anyone how I've bled for
            this house.

LAURA: Course I do.

DEAN: Whey, what am I doing it for? So Mick can
            grief 'is in front of fuckin' kid? People are
            kickin' off. About anythin'. Like. I dunno
            what it is. In town. It the Feathers. They're
            fuckin radge man.

LAURA: What's new?

DEAN: Nah man it's different. Nee-ones happy do
            you know what I mean? They're lookin' for it.

LAURA: So let them.

DEAN: But they sayin' Mick. Ees name. They fuckin'
            hate him.

LAURA: And we love him. You love / him.

DEAN: I cannit stand him. I hate him. I hate / him.

DEAN hitting the wall.

LAURA: (*calming*) Alright. Alright.

87

DEAN:	Pushin' 'is out for some little kid.
LAURA:	He's harsher on you. He is. We've noticed.
DEAN:	It's gettin' worse man. It's your lad makin' it worse.
LAURA:	How could he? (*holding him as he tries to grab her*) You're hurtin' 'is Dean.
DEAN:	It's Mick. He's fuckin' in me head man. I listened to 'im. I believed him. But ees just fuckin' messin' with 'is. Keepin' 'is here like ees fuckin' guard dog.
LAURA:	You protect wer. All o' wer.
DEAN:	Why so he can treat 'is like shit. I'm not havin' it. I'm not.
LAURA:	But it's not Dummey's fault.
DEAN:	It's him makin' it happen. Ee shouldn't be hangin' around him.
SYLV:	(*O.S.*) I'm comin' down.

He opens the door.

DEAN:	When you see what I see man. It's not right.
LAURA:	It's you who's not right.
DEAN:	Fuckin' get rid of him. Or I will.

DEAN exits. SYLV enters, wearing her Chinese dressing gown.

SYLV:	What's going on?

No answer.

LAURA: I was just talking to.

SYLV opens the front door. Unlocks it. Peers out.

SYLV: Who? Disappeared, has he?

LAURA: It was Dean. He was just here.

Beat. SYLV gently closes the door.

SYLV: I don't believe you. (*beat*) We've done this haven't we?

LAURA: This time /

SYLV: / This time it's true? Don't think I can't get rid of you.

LAURA: Had on.

SYLV: You've got no reason to be here have you? Nice home. Good family.

LAURA: It was.

SYLV: You won't bring the outside into my home again. Whatever just happened, happened for the last time. You don't invite boys here. You don't have boys here. You're lucky to still be here after last time. (*as Laura goes to speak*) No. You don't open this door to anyone. Not ever.

LAURA: Oh, for God's sake man. It's not a prison. You cannit just make up rules.

SYLV: In my house…

LAURA: That's it isn't no-one knows the rules. One law for Dummey, one for me. What about Shel'?

SYLV: What about Shel'? You should thank every lucky star you're not Shelley. You want her rules? (*pause*) Pet. You're selling yourself.

LAURA: I'm what?

SYLV: You think I don't understand that 'gratification'. (*of her look*) What? What would an old, sterile, bag like me know about sex? You're a woman now pet, don't look to men to tell you. These clothes. This 'act'. Pushin' it right in tha face so you control it? Flower. It's all a lot less interesting than you imagine. And you'll regret it. I did. Do.

LAURA: (*quietly*) I'm not lying.

SYLV: Christ. (*realising mid-line*) Why would Dean need to talk to you?

LAURA: People are talking.

Beat.

SHELLEY enters.

SHELLEY: Alright. Why yous standing here? It's weird.

SYLV: Lock the door.

SYLV exits.

SHELLEY: We never lock the door.

SHELLEY sits. Pause. LAURA sits next to her.

LAURA:	Dummey kissed us. Do you wanna kna what happened?
SHELLEY:	Nah. Not really.
LAURA:	He kissed us.
SHELLEY:	D'ee touch he your tit?
LAURA:	One of them.
SHELLEY:	Did he get a semi?
LAURA:	Probably. Couldn't tell.
SHELLEY:	That's a bad sign, isn't it?
LAURA:	Shut up. It was dark.
SHELLEY:	Was it what you wanted?
LAURA:	I dunno do I?
SHELLEY:	Did it make you feel attractive?
LAURA:	Shelley man shut up.
SHELLEY:	What?
LAURA:	You ask proper weird questions you like.
SHELLEY:	Sorry.
LAURA:	It's OK. He knocked me teeth like. I've gotta go. Me Mam's doing wer 'family' tea. I have to be there.
SHELLEY:	What's a 'family' tea?
LAURA:	It'll be weird. (*beat*) Do you ever go home Shelley?

SHELLEY: Nah.

LAURA: You stayin' for tea?

SHELLEY: Sylv's put a Chicago mini deep pan in the freezer for 'is.

LAURA: She looks after you, doesn't she?

SHELLEY: Now who's askin' weird questions?

LAURA: Sos I'm bein' gay.

SHELLEY: Don't say that.

LAURA: OK. (*beat*) See you on Shel'.

SHELLEY: Aye see you on Lau.

SCENE 7

DUMMEY, the 'driver' and MICK, the 'passenger' on the settee next to each other. There are three bricks as peddles. MICK is dressed like Toad of Toad Hall. Both are wearing driving gloves and goggles. As MICK gives instructions DUMMEY mimes the movement. DUMMEY holds a wheel.

MICK: Mirrors?

DUMMEY: I've done it!

MICK: Clutch down. Gear in neutral.

DUMMEY: Right.

MICK: No left foot.

DUMMEY: No, I mean right right. Not right left.

MICK: It's left, right? Ha!

DUMMEY rolls his eyes.

MICK: First. Keeping your foot on the clutch. Ignition.

DUMMEY: I haven't got a key.

MICK: (*producing an elaborate one*) Here. Key to the kingdom.

DUMMEY: Take me foot off now?

MICK: Hang about. Slowly lift it until you hear the speed drop. Then push it back. That's the biting point. Again.

MICK makes the engine noise and places his hand on DUMMEY's back, mimicking the vibrations.

MICK: Feel that?

DUMMEY: (*getting into it*) Yeah.

MICK: Now this is the tough bit. Remember CBA. Lift your foot up from the clutch.

DUMMEY: C.

DUMMEY Lightly press down on the accelerator.

DUMMEY: A.

MICK: Easy with the clutch.

MICK bolts forward. Stalled her. Too quick.

DUMMEY: Eh? I did it slowly. That's stupid. You can't just make it up.

MICK: You think I'm gonna let you drive the second love of my life when you're stalling an imaginary car?

DUMMEY: Fine. CBA. CBA. C. A.

MICK: (*holds DUMMEY's legs for the first part*) Gently does it. That's it. Good lad. And we're off.

DUMMEY: Am I driving?

MICK: Yeah lad you are. Clutch foot off.

DUMMEY: How fast am I going?

MICK: About 5 miles an hour.

DUMMEY: Oh.

MICK: You wanna open her up?

DUMMEY: Ye-eah.

MICK: Right you are. Ease off the A. C on. 2nd. And ease it off.

DUMMEY: Good?

MICK: Perfecto.

DUMMEY: Where we going?

MICK: Anywhere you want son. 3rd. Very good. Oh. Blue lights. Ruddy pigs. "Mind your own ruddy business!" (*whispers out the side of his mouth*) Step on it.

DUMMEY: 4th gear?

MICK: Go! (*makes a walkie-talkie sound, into his shoulder, U.S Accent*) Blue Squadron, blue squadron we have a rogue Porsche on Main street, travelling in 5th gear.

DUMMEY: Done! He's chasing wer!

MICK: This is Alpha one requesting back up.

DUMMEY: Faster. Faster.

MICK: (*normal voice*) What we running from again?

DUMMEY: A robbery. A bank. No, a heist. A jewellery one.

MICK: Diamond thieves! (*gangster voice*) They call me Mickey Mystery 'the cat boigler'.

DUMMEY: (*walkie-talkie voice*) Alpha One. Target is on Main Street heading towards the Zoo.

MICK: The zoo?

DUMMEY: I like the zoo.

MICK: No, no, me too me too.

DUMMEY: You said cat burglar.

MICK: Yes, I did. To the lion's den!

DUMMEY: Mind the elephant!

MICK does an elephant noise.

MICK: Families with ice creams!

DUMMEY: Dodgin' 'em.

DUMMEY moves about, bangin' Mick.

MICK: Oi! Me ruddy hip. You're havin' a giraffe here lad.

DUMMEY: Stop changin' your mind! Hold the wheel then.

MICK drives while DUMMEY grabs a giraffe. Bit of improv.

MICK: Could we not of thought of something a bit smaller?

DUMMEY: You keep sayin' it's a convertible. He's heed's oot the top.

MICK: Ha ha! Watch the bend!

DUMMEY turns right quickly and shunts into MICK.

DUMMEY:	Phewf.
MICK:	Cliff edge.
DUMMEY:	Fifty-foot drop. FASTER!
MICK:	There's a gap in the road!
DUMMEY:	We're not gonna make it.
MICK:	We can make it!

They simulate the jump. 'Woooah'.

DUMMEY:	We lost him! See you later pig.
MICK:	That's for Orgreave ye bastards.
DUMMEY:	Eh?
MICK:	Go into that cave.
DUMMEY:	Which cave?
MICK:	THAT CAVE!

DUMMEY slams on the brakes and they both jolt forward and back making the sound of brakes. DUMMEY done with the game.

DUMMEY:	That was good.
MICK:	What's that on your shoulder?
DUMMEY:	Eh?
MICK:	(*whispers out the side of his mouth*) There's something on your shoulder!
DUMMEY:	No there isn't.

MICK: I'll try and pick it off. Hold very still. Close your eyes.

DUMMEY: Why?

MICK: (*normal voice*) We're in a cave mate it's pitch black.

DUMMEY: Oh right.

MICK: (*side of mouth again*) I'm gonna try and brush it off.

DUMMEY, eyes shut, stock still. MICK gets out of the 'Porsche' and tip toes behind DUMMEY.

DUMMEY: Have you got it? Mick? Have you got it? Mick?

At that moment MICK pounces on DUMMEY, tickling him. DUMMEY squeals.

MICK: It's a monster!

They roll around the floor. One on top of the other.

DUMMEY: (*improv*) Get off us man.

SYLV enters.

SYLV: MICKEY.

They startle.

DUMMEY: Hi Sylv.

SYLV: What's this?

DUMMEY: Mick's teaching us how to drive the Porsche before we go out.

SYLV:	It's past five.
DUMMEY:	It's only four thirty. Mick tell her.
SYLV:	Excuse me. Tell her what?
MICK:	Ah Sylv come on.
SYLV:	Home.

DUMMEY takes off his driving gloves and goggles.

DUMMEY:	See yous later.
MICK:	See you tomorrow Sterling. Hey. Stick the giraffe in the garage.
DUMMEY:	OK Mickey Mystery.

DUMMEY exits.

SYLV:	Mickey Mystery?
MICK:	Just a game. We were playing.
SYLV:	On the Porsche?
MICK:	Well. (*he picks up the brick*) Not quite. Couldn't get her through the door.
SYLV:	I can't imagine how he must make you feel.
MICK:	Plum tuckered. He's an energetic little so and so.
SYLV:	You got another chance. I envy you.
MICK:	That's ruddy daft talk that love.
SYLV:	I do. I'll never feel it like you have.

MICK: Hey hey now. What's all this?

SYLV: I thought it was the right thing. Y'know. He loves you.

MICK: You know me, I'm a lovable rogue.

SYLV: I love you very much.

MICK: It's a ruddy love-in then.

They kiss.

SYLV: If the loss I feel about a bloody group of cells/

MICK: / Come on. Don't say that.

SYLV: Is even a tenth of. Shit. It must be confusing.

MICK: You're confusing.

He tries to kiss her again. She's trying to get through.

SYLV: We smother what happened to Michael, we don't forget it.

MICK: Do you wanna tea?

He gets up.

SYLV: But playing it all out again. (*he's off again*) Pet? Christ, will ye, sit down. (*beat. he does*) Michael's there, and here and. Every minute. I know that. And by some twisted bloody miracle ees doppelganger, has just parachuted into wer living room, Pet I don't blame you for taking a 'shine' to him but.

MICK walks away.

100

MICK: Not havin' that.

SYLV: I stood by you, holding your hand, my head up, in the fuckin' Rose and Crown, as people said the most unholy things to me about you, don't you dare make me one of them.

MICK stops.

SYLV: WE choose the house built on sand.

MICK: 'Scuse me the ruddy sermon.

SYLV: WE choose this. (*pointing at the door*) And if they don't like it? Stuff 'em. But why be so clumsy? Where's Dean gonna go when he's finally sick of you?

MICK: It'll be good riddance.

SYLV: And Shelley? Does she deserve to lose us?

MICK: You're punishing me because you're still angry at Michael.

SYLV: This isn't about me.

MICK: You never forgave he wasn't yours!

SYLV: When Michael, God rest / him

MICK: / Went missing.

SYLV: It's not 'missing' pet.

MICK: M.I.A.

SYLV: I should've just organised a funeral. / I should've...

MICK:	Missing. In. Action. Not dead.
SYLV:	Well this bairn certainly isn't him.
MICK:	He's more me than you are.
SYLV:	What? We can't resuscitate Michael out of guilt.
MICK:	I begged him not to go.
SYLV:	You frightened him not to go.
MICK:	So, it's my ruddy fault? (*MICK lashes out at something*) IT'S MY FAULT?
SYLV:	No. Shit. No.
	It's not about faults. It's. Christ do I have to spell it out?
MICK:	I've loved no one more. Not in my life.
SYLV:	Oh, I know. Believe me. I know. You smothered him half to death…

SYLV stops.

SYLV:	Can you not see what the world sees? They're just waiting for one little crack in the armour. This town is gaggin' to mourn that lad for a hero, deify us, they don't want a messy little house like ours spoiling the story.
MICK:	My son is nothin' to do with them.
SYLV:	They hate you for being different and they hate that you have their kids dripping off you. You push Dean out towards them, for

	some silly little boy and you open the floodgates to God knows what.
MICK:	That 'silly boy' needs me.
SYLV:	I need you. This is my home. You're my husband. And you're not being careful.
MICK:	Careful?
SYLV:	This boy is not your son. Nor is Dean, nor anyone else /
MICK:	/ Dummey needs a father. He needs me.
SYLV:	But we don't need you two rolling around on the floor together.

Beat.

MICK:	Fuck you.

He goes upstairs. SYLV remains. Head on the door. She locks the door and draws the curtain.

SCENE 8.

DUMMEY and SHELLEY, in the living room, have a pack of mixed condoms in a paper bag.

DUMMEY: And they just give you them free?

SHELLEY: Aye the' call it a 'one stop shop'.

DUMMEY: Like the 8 till late?

SHELLEY: Aye but these don't have sweets and tabs, they've got chlamydia and washing machines. That one's chocolate. And there's a chilli one an all.

DUMMEY: Will it not sting?

SHELLEY: Why what you gonna do with it?

DUMMEY: Well. What's the tastiest one?

SHELLEY: It's yer cock in a rubber bag Dummey, it's not ready steady cook.

DUMMEY: What's this one then?

SHELLEY: (*reading*) Ribbed for her pleasure. It's not. They rip. It should be 'ripped for her pregnancy'.

DUMMEY: What about this?

SHELLEY: That's yellow.

DUMMEY: Yellow?

SHELLEY: For decoration?

DUMMEY: I don't understand it me. How do you see or taste anything down there?

SYLV enters. She goes straight to the window, peering out. DUMMEY pockets the condoms.

SHELLEY: Why you looking out the window Sylv?

SYLV: It's my window I thought I'd make use of it.

SHELLEY: What you scared of?

SYLV: Funny question.

SHELLEY: You look scared.

SYLV: Maybe I am.

DUMMEY: Who you scared of?

SYLV: Not entirely sure.

DUMMEY: If I was you I wouldn't be scared of anything. You've got Clark, Mick, Dean.

SYLV: Thank Goodness for all those big men.

DUMMEY: Well. Aye.

SHELLEY: She was joking.

SYLV: Do you think I need protecting?

DUMMEY: Well.

SYLV: Have you seen Dean? Have you seen him this week?

Beat.

DUMMEY: He's not been here when I've been here.

SYLV: Funny that. (*beat*) I'm going to say something that you might not like, you might not understand it. Do you hear? But I say it because it's best and I won't argue about it. I think you should stay at home.

DUMMEY: When?

SYLV: I don't think you should pay us quite s'many visits pet, y'understand?

DUMMEY: I don't understand.

SYLV: We're not an open house.

DUMMEY: You mean I'm not allowed?

SYLV: I mean it's best.

DUMMEY: What have I done wrong? (*beat*) I can't. They hate 'is at home.

SYLV: Every bairn feels like that.

SHELLEY: I don't.

SYLV: Your parents actually do hate you flower.

SHELLEY: Aye.

DUMMEY: It's not fair!

SYLV: Life isn't fair.

DUMMEY: But everything's better since I've been here / It's helping.

SYLV: Sometimes it just doesn't /

DUMMEY: / It's the best it's ever been /

SYLV: / It just doesn't work out.

DUMMEY: / Please Sylv. Please. Kev's desperate to kick 'is out. He says that th' can't afford 'is.

SYLV: Parent's joke.

DUMMEY: He says he only keeps 'is to nick stuff from school. That's not a joke. School wants rid of 'is an' all. Sayin' I'm not 'right' for that school. The' never wanted 'is.

SYLV: I'm sure that's true.

DUMMEY: Now you don't want 'is. Fuck's sake. Nee one does. Nee one wants us.

DUMMEY upset. SYLV Passes Dummey a cigarette / glass of alcohol. Pause.

SHELLEY: Can we speak again? Are you upset still?

SYLV: Shelley.

SHELLEY: I waited.

DUMMEY: I'm not upset.

SHELLEY: Why you crying then?

DUMMEY: Got smoke in me eye.

SHELLEY: But the smoke's gannin' the other way.

SYLV: Shelley that's enough. When I was your age nobody wanted me. I felt just like you. But I didn't have a mother. I didn't even have a Kev. Do you know I had eleven sets of parents?

107

DUMMEY: Eleven?

SYLV: Eleven. Passed from pillar to post. And I was cross about it. Ooh. Just like you are now. I hated them for not wanting me. So, I got very angry and did some silly jobs. I tried to have my own family. But. Do you know what I would've done to convince them to take me back? You say it's easier at home since you've been comin' here? There's no reason that has to stop.

DUMMEY: But why?

SHELLEY: Why does he have to go Sylv?

SYLV: Because sometimes the people with the loudest voices win.

SHELLEY: So, are you sayin' you've got a loud voice? Is my voice quiet?

DUMMEY: Who's got a loud voice?

SYLV: (*sad. Sighs*) Not me as it turns out.

DUMMEY: Mick!

SYLV: What about him?

DUMMEY: We're supposed to be riding the Porsche!

SYLV: I'm sorry pet it looks like he's forgotten.

SHELLEY: He wouldn't forget that.

SYLV: He has. He's running errands for me.

DUMMEY: He'll be angry.

SYLV: Nonsense.

DUMMEY: He'll forget about 'is.

SYLV: He will not. Mickey is a lot of things. Sometimes very silly but he's as loyal as that stupid dog of his.

SHELLEY: And he loves you. Yer ees favourite.

DUMMEY: (*delighted*) Am I?

SYLV: No, I am. Now off you go.

SHELLEY: Laura wanted Dummey to go to the next level. (*to DUMMEY*) She doesn't mean upstairs. She means poking her. (*back to SYLV*) Have you told her not to come too?

DUMMEY: Is Laura not comin' back either?

SYLV: This isn't question time.

DUMMEY: What'll I do about Laura?

SYLV: You'll have to put a knot in it. Now go. Out.

SHELLEY: Has Dean gone for good?

SYLV: I sincerely hope not.

SHELLEY: Have you spoken to him?

Beat.

SYLV: No.

SHELLEY: (*realising*) He's why Laura's not here too.

SYLV: Laura shouldn't have been here in the first place.

SHELLEY: Is she banish'ed?

SYLV: It's my house. Mine. Or had you forgotten as you're here so often?

SHELLEY: Where am I supposed to go? (*beat*) What about Mick though? Dummey has to keep coming for Mick. Cos he'll miss him Sylv. He will. Mick's changed cos of Dummey. He's /

SYLV: / Give it a rest Shelley FOR FUCK'S SAKE.

Beat. Kids taken aback.

SYLV: He's not staying. Do you understand? And if you keep on at 'is. You'll be next.

SHELLEY: But I can't go.

Guilt ridden SYLV goes to the door. Pre-occupied, she opens it. Shuts it. Locks it. Walks upstairs.

DUMMEY: Sorry Sylv. For whatever I've done…

What have I done?

Pause

Have you ever heard her swear like that before?

SHELLEY: Not at me.

DUMMEY: Did you know that thing about her having so many parents?

SHELLEY: Nah.

DUMMEY: Do you think it's weird?

SHELLEY: Haven't thought about it.

(*pause*) Everythin's changing.

DUMMEY: (*kindly*) She won't chuck you out Shel'.

SHELLEY: She never spoke to 'is like that. Never.

DUMMEY: She was just annoyed.

SHELLEY: I don't understand.

DUMMEY: I do. (*he gets up*) It's what happens. When I hang around too long. Things fuck up.

Beat. He goes to the door.

SHELLEY: Do you want 'is to walk you back cos you're sad?

DUMMEY: Nah you're alreet.

He opens the door.

SHELLEY: Do you want some tabs cos you can't get served?

DUMMEY: Nah.

SHELLEY: Do you want / 'is to

DUMMEY: See you later Shel'.

SHELLEY: I'll tell Laura. She might talk to you at school.

DUMMEY smiles. She's not a good liar.

DUMMEY: She won't. See you on.

SHELLEY doesn't reply. Then; as he goes.

SHELLEY: Dummey. Thanks. For being me friend.

SCENE 9

Empty room. 3 days later.

KETTLE sound. Children playing football on a field not far away. DEAN walks down the stairs and into the LIVING ROOM in a tracksuit and vest. He walks past the tank and taps on the bench underneath. He exits to KITCHEN and returns with a TEA. Looks around and takes the place in as he drinks it. He feeds the snake, taking a mouse out just as in SCENE 1, taking out VIVIAN LEIGH if possible. He strokes her. MICK enters from UPSTAIRS but slows on seeing DEAN. Watches DEAN and enters the ROOM. They acknowledge each other frostily. MICK looks a bit lost and is pacing around. He moves to the WINDOW staring out.

DEAN:	She's at church.
MICK:	What?
DEAN:	She's at church. (*beat*) Sylv.

Beat.

MICK:	Sylv? She's er. At church.

Beat.

DEAN:	Waiting on the bairn?
MICK:	You what?
DEAN:	Haven't seen 'im.
MICK:	Three days.
DEAN:	Probably at the football.
MICK:	What?

DEAN:	There's a match on at the field. Geet mad all the kids together match. They're loving it. All pilin' in. (*beat*) The bairn's probably at that. (*beat*) Or homework. (*beat*) Maybes ees been telt. (*MICK looks at DEAN*) Not to come. You kna. By ees Mam or whatever.

MICK frowns. Suspicious. He is down. DEAN senses it.

DEAN:	She's feedin' better. (*no response*) Vivian Leigh. She's eating again.

MICK:	Oh. Yes. The... er vet sorted the erm. Thing.

DEAN:	She's eating at proper times. That's what it is.

MICK at the window. Not listening really. FOOTBALL still heard outside.

DEAN:	Her stomach's been fucked with all the mental feeding. She's been owerfed ye kna. But now she's better an' that, on the mend y'kna, cos she's. Back to normal.

MICK:	(*at the window watching the football game*) Who are you when you're at home? Terry Nutkins?

DEAN:	Eh?

MICK:	(*turns. Sharp*) You've fed the fucker properly. Congratulations. What d'ye want a fuckin' medal?

Beat. DEAN putting the PYTHON back.

MICK:	Cost enough. Private ruddy medicine. Not made of money you know. (*trails off*)

Beat.

DEAN: Worth it though. To get her back to normal.
               Thanks. For the vets.

*He motions to leave. Atmosphere has turned cold. MICK attempts
reconciliation.*

MICK: What kind of kid calls a snake Vivian ruddy
               Leigh?

DEAN: Eh?

MICK: You lot. Most kids'd call it killer, or hiss, or
               ruddy Keegan at least. But Vivian Leigh!

DEAN: The first idea was just call it snake. Or long.

MICK: Jesus that's some ruddy focus group. Now
               we've got a ruddy snake here lads, it's long
               and it's a snake now can anyone think of
               anything to call it? Anything at all. It's a long
               snake.

DEAN: I never thought about it but Vivian Leigh is
               a weird name. For a snake like.

MICK: Weird? It's kids who are obsessed with 'Gone
               with the Wind' is weird. Most kids wanna
               watch ruddy Terminator.

DEAN: I used to love it.

MICK: Bloomin' weird kid. Imagine your family
               comin' here then and seein' you watchin'
               Gone with the ruddy wind.

DEAN: Would've battered 'is.

MICK: (*smiling and reminiscing*) Ruddy hell. Snake.
               And Long. Jesus.

DEAN:	Ye kna that happened with that car.
MICK:	Eh?
DEAN:	They had a what'd you caal them groups?
MICK:	Focus groups.
DEAN:	Aye them'uns. Whey the had a Focus group once for the new Ford car.
MICK:	Don't tell me.
DEAN:	Aye they came up with two names. Focus.
MICK:	And Kaa. Jesus ruddy Christ.
DEAN:	Me and Michael could've worked for Ford after all.

Mood sobers at the talk of Michael. SHELLEY enters form the front door. Stops immediately. Beat.

DEAN: Alreet Shel'.

No answer. Beat. DEAN makes sure the snake is OK. Closes up the tank if he hasn't already. SHELLEY hasn't moved. MICK sat.

MICK:	Hello darlin'.
SHELLEY:	(*loud*) I've just seen a Porsche.
MICK:	What kind of Porsche girl?
SHELLEY:	Like yours.
DEAN:	Hear that? Canny rare.
MICK:	Are ye sure girl?

116

DEAN: Do yous wanna tea or owt?

DEAN leaves to the KITCHEN.

MICK: No.

SHELLEY: Nah. (*hushed*) It's Dummey.

MICK: What's he ruddy doin? Playin at James ruddy Bond?

DEAN: (*O.S.*) I'll make one anyways.

SHELLEY: I've been trying to tell you but I'm not supposed to say.

MICK: What?

SHELLEY: I can't betray Sylv but she changed everything. She's banned Dummey. For the best. And Laura. Because of you.

MICK: She's done ruddy what... Best?

SHELLEY: She didn't want to do it.

MICK: Oh she wanted t' do it.

SHELLEY: Dummey was gutted but ees so used to rejection he just went. He might be havin' a breakdown, or a fit, or he might like try and punch a wall, or ees Mam or anythin'.

MICK: Alright alright. Focus. Where is he? Get him here. No ruddy. No. Hang on. This'll need covert /

SHELLEY: It wasn't Sylv's idea.

MICK: You what?

117

SHELLEY: Sylv was worried… about people.

MICK: Ah ruddy hell not this.

SHELLEY: No. Dean is people. Dean told Sylv, he made her choose. Sylv said he was sayin' all sorts. She got proper scared and took it out on me. Now she's banished everyone.

MICK: The little bastard!

SHELLEY: So I've got no-one.

MICK: Bastard. Dean? (*beat. Realising he's been heard*) Dean?

Sound of the back door closing.

SCENE 10

Darkness. DUMMEY 'enters'. The lights suddenly burst on. The LIVING ROOM is chaotic and full of smoke. A party has been organised by MICK to celebrate DUMMEY's 'graduation' at the house. The set looks dishevelled and anarchic. SYLV is not there. SHELLEY is drinking Vodka, wearing a sombrero as a party hat, SHELLEY gets through three bottles throughout the scene. LAURA is on the floor. She is wearing her best outfit, possibly a naval cap and applying SYLV's make up to her own face. Her mirror is being propped up by an exotic Mexican dildo. On the table, there are biscuits and alcohol. There is a crude banner over the fire place. It reads 'Commissioning Ball' spelled incorrectly. MICK is wearing a military cap and has a sword.

ALL:　　　　*(led by Mick, the girls get it slightly wrong)* Happy

LAURA:　　　What is it?

ALL:　　　　Sovereign's Parade!

MICK:　　　　Here he is! Our boy.

During the following MICK strides over and places the cap on Dummey's head, saluting him to amused looks from the group.

MICK:　　　　Top Officer Cadet Dummett. I present to you, the sword of honour.

Girls clap. DUMMEY struggles with the sword.

MICK:　　　　*(conducting)* Altogether.

ALL:　　　　For he's a jolly good fellow, for he's a jolly good fellow, for he's a jolly good fe-eh-low. Which nobody can deny. And so say all of us.

119

DUMMEY laughs, chuffed and surprised with his hero's welcome.

MICK: How does it feel Second Lieutenant?

DUMMEY: What's this?

MICK: Your ruddy graduation man!

DUMMEY: Graduation? (*to SHELLEY*) Has Sylv?

MICK: Mind you could've made an effort, look at the state of this kit! No time for your BoHo chic here son.

MICK tucks DUMMEY's shirt in for him.

DUMMEY: Am I back in?

SYLV enters through the front door, in a red coat.

MICK: (*sings*) / Never seen you lookin' so lovely as you did / tonight.

SYLV: What on earth

MICK: LADY IN RED. Is dancing with me.

He dances with SYLV.

SYLV: Stop it.

MICK: Cheek to cheek.

SYLV: What's this?

MICK: It's a party and I'll cry if you don't want to.

LAURA: It's ees graduation ceremony Sylv.

SYLV: I see you're back.

MICK:	(*stoic, wiping pretend tears away*) Our little laddie in the big wide world. A proud moment for any mother. Someone grab the ruddy Kleenex.
SYLV:	And now you're finishing up?
MICK:	Quite Right. That's enough of the formal stuff. It's ball time! Not that kind of ball! You dirty minded scoundrels! We Lieutenant, me and you, you and me, are off for a spin. Prepare the Batmobile!
SYLV:	Mickey.
MICK:	Sylv man relax.
SYLV:	Alan do you have something you'd like to say to Mickey?
MICK:	We want the wind rushing through the ol' hair. The evening sunshine pouring through me helmet. You know I got a compliment on my driving this very day.
DUMMEY:	Did you?
MICK:	Yep. A little note left on me windscreen. Parking fine.
DUMMEY:	Ha!
SHELLEY:	(*groans, drinks more*)
SYLV:	(*to SHELLEY*) We need to talk.

SHELLEY hasn't said a word.

121

MICK: Not yet. Not yet. Drinks! D.J. Shellsuit, spin your wheels.

SHELLEY plays a loud song on the HI-FI/TV. SYLV draws the curtains. MICK dances. SYLV tries to combat the dishevelled room. She has to play this carefully. They talk loudly over the music.

LAURA: You're a sexy dancer Mick.

MICK: Me? Oh I'm like Fred a-ruddy Staire me.

SHELLEY: More like Fred a-ruddy Stair lift.

MICK: Oi! These hips seemed to work on a few people thank you!

SHELLEY: (*to DUMMEY*) Aye. Before the weight gain.

LAURA: I think it's right sexy.

DUMMEY: Aye you're pretty good for an owd gadgie.

MICK: Enough of the character assassination. Ruddy McCarthy witch hunt this.

LAURA: Dummey, would you teach me?

He hesitates, before LAURA grabs him.

LAURA: Come on. What is it? Dun dun dun dun.

LAURA's version is boringly provocative.

SYLV: Shelley, come here please.

SHELLEY: We need more drink.

SHELLEY goes to the kitchen. SYLV follows.

MICK:	Private. Distraction duty!
LAURA:	(*grabbing the dildo*) I'll ask her how you use this. (*shouting after Sylv*) How sexpert.

Exits.

MICK:	You'll catch a few flies that way. (*he closes DUMMEY's mouth*) Is this a good ceremonial ball?
DUMMEY:	The best.
MICK:	Do you like your hat?
DUMMEY:	Aye. It's a bit big.
MICK:	You'll grow into it. That's my old cap that is.
DUMMEY:	Wow. An antique.
MICK:	Yer Cheeky. It's yours if you want it.
DUMMEY:	I couldn't.
MICK:	You're the young military man in the family aren't you?
DUMMEY:	I didn't go to the cadets. You were right.
MICK:	(*smiles*) How about bein' the Captain o'this house?
DUMMEY:	Do I really have to stop coming?
MICK:	Well that's ruddy gratitude for you!
DUMMEY:	Graduating. Is this about yous wanting us to leave.

MICK: There's gonna be a meeting about that. I'm taking it right to the top office.

DUMMEY: I can stay?

MICK: Son. I'd give them all away if it meant you still coming.

DUMMEY: Really?

MICK: Really. I'm not lettin' you go anywhere. Come here.

They hug. MICK rubs his stubble on DUMMEY's face.

DUMMEY: Ow. Your beard's scratchy.

MICK: (*soppy voice*) Oh well let me kiss it better.

He plants big sloppy kisses on DUMMEY's head. DUMMEY squeals with simultaneous delight and horror. CLARK begins barking from the KITCHEN.

SYLV: (*O.S.*) Clark. Quiet. Stop that.

DUMMEY: Stop it man I'm soaking.

MICK picks him up.

MICK: Ha ha! I love you kid.

LAURA: (*O.S.*) Clark! Ow! He's fuckin' bit 'is

SHELLEY: (*O.S.*) No he hasn't.

SYLV: (*O.S.*) He has!

MICK lowers DUMMEY beneath him and grabs him to tickle him. CLARK still barking.

DUMMEY:	Ah Mick. That's hurting. (*more violent*) Mick man. It hurts.
SYLV:	(*O.S.*) You've wound that dog up crazy you stupid man. Help? Now.

LAURA enters from the KITCHEN, as the others run to the KITCHEN. Noises off throughout, MICK, CLARK, SYLV, SHELLEY.

LAURA:	He nearly took me hand off.
DUMMEY:	Let 'is see then. (*he goes over to her*) I think you'll be OK.
LAURA:	You sayin' I'm bein' a drama queen?
DUMMEY:	No. (*beat*) Without the house, you would'nt be seen talkin' to 'is would ye?
LAURA:	I dunno.
DUMMEY:	Cos it's embarrassin'. Cos of what people'd say.
LAURA:	(*beat*) People'd call you the stinker king. They'd say you were ridin' the town bike.
DUMMEY:	Is that what you are?
LAURA:	Maybe.
DUMMEY:	I wouldn't care if you were.
LAURA:	Yes you would.
DUMMEY:	I wouldn't care what you'd done.
LAURA:	Who. I've done canny stupid stuff.

DUMMEY: Not to me.

LAURA: Nar to me.

DUMMEY: (*beat*) I've got high hopes.

LAURA: Have you?

DUMMEY: I think you're totally lush.

LAURA: (*smiles*) Do you wanna see each other?

DUMMEY: Us? Like. Gan to town and have meals and that?

LAURA: Aye if you want tee.

DUMMEY: Mint. Do you want?

LAURA smiles. Kisses his cheek. Leads him upstairs. He stops.

LAURA: You don't fancy us.

DUMMEY: No. (*beat*) I haven't. Before.

LAURA: Follow me.

SYLV enters as they exit, moves to stop them and MICK grabs her.

SYLV: No way. Not today.

MICK: How else d'you celebrate a ruddy graduation? You're like a ruddy Goth, without the dry wit. This is meant to be a party girl.

SHELLEY staggers in with three empty bottles. Gives one with a drip left to MICK.

SHELLEY: There's not much left.

MICK: Jesus Shelley that's litres you've put away girl.

SHELLEY: Guts of steel Mick.

MICK picks up the dildo like a sword. Grabs a bottle of rum from the cupboard.

MICK: As the fellah on the song says. We're gonna party like it's your birthday and drink Barcadi like it's your birthday. I am the party commander. Who's with me?

SHELLEY: I am!

SHELLEY gets up and crashes into SYLV, taking them into the furniture.

MICK: Woah Shel'. (*grabs her, dildo still in hand, SYLV falls and hurts her arm*) I've got you Shelley.

MICK struggling with SHELLEY. MICK has her from behind. They fall to the floor.

SHELLEY: Did I catch you Sylv? I'm pissed Sylv.

MICK: Straight from the horse's mouth.

SHELLEY: Who you calling a horse?

They laugh.

SYLV: I'm fine thanks Mick.

MICK: I'm right on top of you! (*they both find this hilarious*) We're horsin' around!

MICK and SHELLEY are both laughing, MICK being a rodeo cow boy. DEAN enters.

DEAN:　　　　Look at you man. She's sixteen.

Sobering SHELLEY and MICK. Beat.

MICK:　　　　Excuse me?

DEAN:　　　　Get off her.

MICK:　　　　Now why would you say a thing like that?

DEAN:　　　　(*quietly*) Yous all think it!

MICK:　　　　(*getting up now*) What's that Dean?

SYLV:　　　　What do we all think?

MICK:　　　　Spit it out.

DEAN:　　　　Michael.

Beat.

SYLV:　　　　Shelley go and fetch Laura. It's time to go.

SHELLEY:　　Yes Sylv.

SHELLEY gets herself together and goes. The two men are facing each other. The two men are still physically close. MICK holding DEAN by the face or arms.

MICK:　　　　Don't bring your shit into this house. Ruddy hell what's this the thriller in Manilla?

DEAN:　　　　(*almost playful*) Get off us man.

They stand with MICK holding DEAN. You always wanted old Mick around didn't you? Look at me. Love me. Don't play with the other boys.

SYLV: That's enough.

MICK: You whine about living in a small pond, you're not even a big fish.

DEAN: I've worked y'out.

MICK: What's that Sherlock?

DEAN: I protect you.

MICK: From who? (*of the window*) Your other friends? The Fountain Park Massive? There's no one ruddy there.

DEAN: You'll get a fuckin' shock.

MICK: (*gently slaps DEAN*) Who from Deano lad? Them who spat you out in the first place? They've conned you, you little berk.

SYLV: (*warning*) Mick.

DEAN: You'll get sent down.

MICK: (*Mick slaps him gently again*) Maybe it is time you fucked off. For good. I have suffered you. Hanging around my neck. Like a fucking limpet. Like a disease. It's to my eternal regret that when my brave boy, my selfless good boy, my Michael left us, you remained. Like glue. Like mould.

DEAN: I hate you.

129

MICK: That's not true is it? But you know Dean, ironically, you never meant a ruddy thing to me. You were always second best. Michael's young hanger on. Too much love? That's what they say isn't it, the little mob in your ear? Funny goings on? Except that would mean going near you.

DEAN has had enough. He drives into MICK. With one blow he slams him against the wall. With the other hand he picks him up from the floor and holds him against the wall peering into his face. MICK is shocked. It looks as if DEAN will kill MICK.

SYLV runs in. SHELLEY, DUMMEY and LAURA run down the stairs. LAURA is wearing SYLV's gown. DUMMEY his Captain's hat, school shirt, boxers and socks. Lines can run over each other if needed.

SYLV: What the hell is going on?

DUMMEY: DEAN! Stop.

SYLV: DEAN!

DUMMEY: Let him go!

DUMMEY has run at DEAN. DEAN drops MICK who hits the floor hard. Mick hits his head. DEAN grabs DUMMEY. Not threateningly but with care.

DEAN: He's using you. All of you.

LAURA: Stop it Dean.

DUMMEY trying to break free.

DUMMEY: Get up Mick.

LAURA: What have you done Dean?

DEAN:	He's faking it like everythin' else.
SYLV:	Mickey?
DUMMEY:	Mick. It's me. Get up.
MICK:	(*delirious*) I'm all right son.
DUMMEY:	I'm here.
MICK:	(*tearing*) You came back.

MICK begins to cry.

DEAN:	Stop it. (*to SYLV*) Shut him up.
MICK:	You let them turn on me Son.
DEAN:	He's fuckin' lost it.
SYLV:	Dear Goodness.
MICK:	Why didn't you come back sooner lad?
LAURA:	Dean stop this.
DEAN:	Yous don't get it do you? The club's over. It's finished. The house is finished.

SHELLEY suddenly up, towards DEAN. Knife in hand. DUMMEY free, runs to MICK. Flings himself on top of the crying MICK.

SHELLEY:	I'll kill you.

She points it at DEAN's neck. DEAN frozen. It's our house.

SYLV:	(*loudly*) That's enough. Stop it. All of you.
MICK:	(*whimpers*) My beautiful, darling boy. I forgive you son. I do.

SYLV: ENOUGH! (*carefully*) Pet. Give it over. Come on now. Look. It's OK. Shelley. Look at me. It's OK. Nothing's over. Now give that. Good girl. (*she takes the sharp object*) Alan, let Mick alone now.

DUMMEY: I won't leave him.

SYLV: (*pulling him up with surprising strength*) You already have.

LAURA grabs DUMMEY, protecting him.

SYLV: Mickey? Corporal Dobson. (*he looks*) Michael's gone. He went to fight. He's not coming back to you now. Nor never. That boy's dead.

MICK: No he's not leaving again.

LAURA: We can fix this.

DEAN: What me and you? I told you.

LAURA: You told 'is nowt. You're jealous of him.

DEAN: I've been listenin' to Mick all me life…

LAURA: Remember how you were treated Dean.

DEAN: That's the real world man. Aye it's shit, there's nowt to try for, but at least it's real.

LAURA: Real like your brothers?

SYLV: You walk out that door you'll be locked up, or drugged up within a week.

DEAN: Cannit be any worse.

132

SYLV:	Go on then. What's keepin' you?
DEAN:	(*to group*) What yous gonna do when they bust the hinges in? Divin't have your name attached to this place when it kicks off. The Pied Piper of Fountain Park in the newspapers? Spray paint. Smashed windows. They'll decide.
SYLV:	They've given you nothing.
DEAN:	He's done fuck all for 'is since I was fifteen years old. (*to MICK*) Remember when I was your little'un? Your special lad? When you took me up to the slag to play bows and fucking arrows?
SYLV:	He treated you like a son.
DEAN:	Until I was too old. You're just as bad. Bringing him meat.
LAURA:	It was us brought Dummey in.
DEAN:	Does it keep him calm? Stop him crying? You bring him a lad and you get sex?
SHELLEY:	It was me wanted Dummey here.
DEAN:	She made you think that. (*to SYLV*) Why'd yous all keep it a secret? Eh? Why's everyone not comin' in? (*beat*) No one has the answer. Michael'd rather walk into a death zone than into ee's own house and that's not weird? What about Michael?

SYLV:	Oh, the gospel according to Michael, the one he can't answer cos he's conveniently dead, the one according to the Feathers pub.
DEAN:	Michael Jr. went and tried to get himself blown up.
SYLV:	Maybe.
DEAN:	He smothered him.
SYLV:	Probably yes.
DEAN:	Hangin' about Michael's mates.
SYLV:	Michael left because he was angry.
DEAN:	You don't dee that unless there's somethin' gone on.
SYLV:	Oh now we're into it. The rumour mill.
DEAN:	Whey where does it come from?
SYLV:	Have you never been the subject of a rumour? A nasty rumour that grows from nowhere? Oh I remember wasn't it...
DEAN:	(*wrought aggression*) Fuck off man.
SYLV:	What was it you did again? Laura'll remember, she had a black eye for weeks.
DEAN:	Fuckin' old bitch.
SYLV:	Not so keen on rumours now? Laura?
LAURA:	I don't want to.
DUMMEY:	(*to LAURA*) What happened?

134

SYLV:	Mick loved Michael. That's what happened.
DEAN:	Aye too much. I've seen it with me own eyes man.
SYLV:	Seen what exactly?
DEAN:	I'm not saying he fuckin' touches wer man. He's too pathetic. I'm surprised he gets it up with you.
SYLV:	I should've left you to follow your brothers.
DEAN:	I'm saying he's fuckin' weird. Young'uns hanging off him.
SYLV:	And that's a crime?
DEAN:	It's not right.
SYLV:	So what do you and your new friends actually say pet? (*beat*) Pest? Peado? What's the word?
DEAN:	He shouldn't be around kids.
SYLV:	And that's the truth?
DEAN:	What people think is the truth. Ye wanna talk about lies? Do you want a ride in the Porsche? '1973 911 you cannot ruddy beat her'. Ye kna as well as I dee there's nowt there man. It's fantasy.
DUMMEY:	But the photo!
SHELLEY:	It's from a magazine.
DUMMEY:	You knew?

DEAN: Ees never fitted in. Why's he never had a mate?

DUMMEY: He's got us.

DEAN: Ees fifty years older than you.

SYLV: Having a fake car. Loving you. What is it that you and your friends are actually scared of?

DEAN: Same thing Michael was.

SYLV: The Wizard of Oz crying on the floor?

DEAN: He's not like us.

SYLV: Am I like you? Cos if you crack open that door, some of Fountain Park's finest's coming through it, pitchforks an' all, you said it yourself. Once opinion is decided. No amount of truth's stopping that wave of fear. You open those doors, you draw the spotlight this way, I flee the town I grew up in, which I happen to love. A home which I've built and shared.

DEAN: It's not about you though.

SYLV: You hadn't stopped to think about my problems, had you? Your little temper tantrum shouldn't affect me? All this fuss, for scared little boys.

You might feel 'trapped' here Dean and have fucked away your life but the rest of us aren't to blame.

DEAN:	Whey who is then?
SYLV:	Drugs. Dole. Death. It didn't catch you because you were here, with me. Don't you forget, you came to us. You always have. All of you. We never invited you in, not one.
	We have given so much of ourselves. Because yes, we loved it. But you all kept coming back. In your droves. Hundreds of you. Scared kids, angry kids, lonely kids with nowt better to do. Craving attention, our love, traipsing yer muddy feet into the floor and your dirty little bits on me sheets, in and out, in and out, because you knew you fitted in here. You knew he would love you and mould you and teach you what others wouldn't. You knew the old barren bitch would mother you.
	We'd allow it all, everything you're not allowed. We'd give you everything you crave and we'd serve it on a plate. Free of charge. Now is that wrong?

A noise is heard, possibly the sound of a smashed window

Is that wrong Dean?

Beat. DEAN in conflict. LAURA goes towards him.

LAURA:	It isn't Dean.
SYLV:	This is our Home.
LAURA:	It's the best thing's ever happened to 'wer.

Beat. DEAN still doesn't know what to do next, he's holding the door handle. LAURA touches his arm.

DUMMEY: It's my fault. It's me who shouldn't be here. (*to SYLV*) You were right Sylv.

(*back to Dean, slowly*) I just wanted to keep seein' Mick. And if I went, you'd stay. Wouldn't you?

DEAN lets go of the handle.

DEAN: Aye.

DUMMEY: I'll go.

DEAN nods and reacts. Then out of nowhere.

MICK: (*to DUMMEY*) No son.

DEAN exits. SYLV sighs, exhausted.

SYLV: Time to go.

SYLV exhales and then crumples. It only lasts a few beats before she is wiping away any tears and stoically inhaling and breathing.

SYLV: Oh Mickey. (*she goes to MICK who for the last passage has been shell shocked. Out of it*) Oh darling you've cut your head there. (*SYLV pulls a tissue from her sleeve and licks it. She dabs MICK's head. The kids stand motionless*)

Shelley fetch 'is a cloth.

SHELLEY: Do you not want a plaster for a cut?

SYLV: Cloth, plaster, just do it.

SHELLEY is in shock, she doesn't move from her seat. LAURA goes.

SYLV: Mickey? Lover? I need you to move darling. I need you to help me.

He does nothing. LAURA returns with a wet flannel.

SYLV: (*heaving MICK with all her might up from the floor*) C'mon. (*they stagger a pace or two but SYLV can't move him*) I can't do it on me own.

SYLV is dropping MICK. LAURA helps.

LAURA: Here.

LAURA helps SYLV and they haul him to the settee and drop him just in front of it. LAURA props a cushion behind him. Exhausted, SYLV walks over to her chair and sits down.

LAURA: I think it's time to go.

SHELLEY doesn't move

SHELLEY: Where?

Beat. LAURA and DUMMEY go to the door. LAURA stops.

LAURA: I never knew Michael was dead. I always thought he'd come back cos he fancied 'is. You know how when you're a kid you think you've got a chance with someone much older? I had that. Stupid isn't it?

SYLV: Not the time pet.

LAURA: He used to nick 'is sweets from the shop.

SYLV: Give it a rest Laura man.

LAURA: When he left I was here. I said are you scared to go and he said nah. I said why you going then? He said Sylv's showed 'is the way out. I never understood it then.

SYLV is silent.

LAURA: I bet he was grateful Sylv. If you did.

SYLV is breaking.

DUMMEY still has MICK's hat in his hands.

DUMMEY: Mick?

LAURA: We have to go.

DUMMEY: I just wanna say goodbye.

LAURA: (*carefully, adult*) I think that's it.

DUMMEY: (*beat. Nods / understands. Turns back to MICK. Beat*) Mick. Mick. Corporal.

MICK looks up. Glazed. DUMMEY hands him the hat. MICK takes it. DUMMEY forces a smile out, through his tearing eyes.

DUMMEY: There's your ruddy hat.

DUMMEY forces a smile as he hands over the hat.

MICK stares at the hat.

All kids exit.

SOUNDSCAPE of the danger to come. Sirens, eggs, voices, dogs, smashed window, a knock at the door.

END.